making *dead birds* chronicle of a film

making *dead birds*

chronicle of a film

robert gardner

foreword by phillip lopate

edited by charles warren
designed by jeannet leendertse

peabody museum press
harvard university

Editorial direction: Joan K. O'Donnell
Production supervision: Donna Dickerson
Printed and bound in Singapore on acid-free paper by Tien Wah Press.

ISBN 978-0-87365-823-2

Library of Congress Cataloging-in-Publication Data

Gardner, Robert, 1925-
  Making Dead birds : chronicle of a film / Robert Gardner ; foreword by Phillip Lopate ; edited by Charles Warren ; designed by Jeannet Leendertse.
     p. cm.
  Includes bibliographical references.
  ISBN 978-0-87365-823-2 (alk. paper)
  1. Dani (New Guinean people)--Social life and customs. 2. Ethnographic films--New Guinea. 3. Dead birds (Motion picture) 4. New Guinea--Social life and customs. I. Warren, Charles, 1948- II. Title.
  DU744.35.D32G37 2007
  305.89'912--dc22

                        2007025341

Peabody Museum Press
Peabody Museum of Archaeology and Ethnology
Harvard University
11 Divinity Avenue
Cambridge. MA 02138
www.peabody.harvard.edu/publications

For Adele, and for my children

Robert Gardner filming ritual battle

contents

Gardner pondering the changing tide of a ritual battle

foreword: a voyage to the self

by phillip lopate

In 1964, the year I turned twenty-one and graduated from college, Lyndon B. Johnson had just assumed the presidency after John F. Kennedy's assassination, we were in the thick of the Cold War, Patrice Lumumba had been unseated by a CIA coup and killed in the Congo, the recent Cuban missile crisis still raised a shiver of apocalyptic foretaste, and the first American troops had been sent as "advisors" to Vietnam. It was a nervous time and yet an idealistic one. Joining Mississippi Freedom Summer, signing up for the Peace Corps, waging revolutionary armed struggle, or making socially engaged art all seemed valid ways to help bring about a better world.

In the precarious mood of 1964, Robert Gardner released his documentary feature *Dead Birds*, a film that reflected both the violence and the hope of the time. It remains projected still, however subliminally, on our culture's mind-screen.

In retrospect, *Dead Birds* can be seen as a crossover film, dividing all that preceded and followed it in filmmaking. Never had there been so compelling a model of ethnographic cinema. Previously there had been popular, colorful, but anthropologically naïve documentaries about peoples of the wild, such as *Nanook of the North* and *Grass*, as well as scrupulously accurate ethnographic shorts made by such distinguished anthropologists as Margaret Mead and Gregory Bateson. John Marshall had shot thousands of feet of film on the Bushmen of the Kalahari Desert; he and Gardner together edited the footage into *The Hunters* (1958), an informative and genial episodic film that expanded the ethnographic short documentary to feature length.

Dead Birds was something else entirely: a powerful, compact story of chilling relevance about the Dani, a neolithic farmer-warrior group in New Guinea that practiced one-for-one revenge-based warfare with a neighboring rival tribe. The film showed how these likable and friendly (to the film crew, anyway) people believed that the universe was out of balance unless they could get even, homicidally speaking, with the other tribe. Because that other tribe believed the same, individual losses on each side were avenged with reciprocal murders, either by doing battle openly or by sneaking up on an unsuspecting enemy—a child, a woman, an old man; it didn't matter—who had wandered into no-man's-land.

The narrative of *Dead Birds* was organized around a few key protagonists: the Dani warrior Weyak, who daily mounted a watchtower to keep an eye on the enemy, and the young boy Pua, who herded pigs when not distracted by daydreams. Some of the most memorable images in the film are the battle scenes and the funerals, scenes in which lines of warriors taunt each other and pigs are slaughtered with bow and arrow at close range. If all this "primitive" bloodletting seemed senseless, was it any more senseless than the periodic massacres occurring in so-called civilized society? *Dead Birds* asked us to ponder the nature and function of human aggression by watching it operate in a highly controlled, ritualized, and, in a way, humanely limited circumstance—in which a single death was usually sufficient to stop the killing for a while.

"Of the mountain of letters, journals, camera notes, articles, interviews, and reviews," wrote Robert Gardner in 2004, "it is my solemn intention to some day consider it all in a written account of the film's making." Hence this book, which traces the struggle to create *Dead Birds*. In documentary filmmaking, the period of fundraising and preparation usually far exceeds the actual shooting time. Here, we are given an inside glimpse of the patience and persistence necessary to drill through the layers of governmental and charitable bureaucracy required to get such a project off the ground.

Gardner, trained as both anthropologist and filmmaker, took great pains to honor alike the scientific and artistic parts of the venture. But he was inclined from the start toward a humanistic, almost belletristic, anthropology that valued subjective perceptions, intuitions, and experiences. He and his team tried to learn as much of the language and circumstances of the Dani as they could before setting off for New Guinea, and he spent enough time with the people to ensure that his film about them would not be a shallow, hit-and-run documentary. He also surrounded himself with professionals whose perspectives would inform and check his own. The team included still photographer Eliot Elisofon, Dutch anthropologist Jan Broekhuyse, writer Peter Matthiessen, anthropology graduate student Karl Heider, soundman/photographer Michael Rockefeller, and, briefly, medical student Samuel Putnam and botanist Chris Versteegh.

During his months with the Dani, Gardner pondered how he might organize the overflow of impressions and information into a single cohesive story. In this, his first major film project, he sought a ruling metaphor that would convey his core understanding of the people under scrutiny— as he would in his later films *Rivers of Sand, Forest of Bliss,* and *Ika Hands*. Before he left New Guinea, he found his metaphor in the fact that the Dani identify deeply with birds and refer to their victims' captured weapons, ornaments, and corpses by the term "dead birds." From the outtakes of footage presented in a DVD of the movie, it is clear that Gardner decided to exclude numerous sequences and subplots that would not fit into this theme of mortality and revenge killing.

In many respects, the Dani in the film do not come across as a particularly bloodthirsty people. They seem charming and reasonable, self-contained yet spontaneous—both in the film and in Gardner's diaries, letters, and notes about them. All the more appalling, then, that their very identity—especially that of the men—seems to hinge on the spilling of blood. For the most part, Gardner's point of view is that this was the "reality" of the situation. So scrupulous was his refusal to try to deter the Dani from warfare that the rumor spread to the outside world that he and his team were provoking a war for the sake of filming it. Was this amoral spectatorship, or scientific detachment?

As the following pages show, the filmmaker's attitude toward the Dani's ritual warfare was complicated. On the one hand, he was rightfully indignant when false reports circulated that he and his crew had instigated the fighting, and the documents presented here show the lengths to which he went to quell these allegations. He knew that he was documenting a way of life that had gone on probably for centuries; in no way was he the cause of it. On the other hand, because he had chosen the ritualized vendetta as the subject of his film, he clearly had an expectation, if not a desire, that the fighting continue. No warfare, no film.

Thus, when Margaret Mead counseled Gardner against making a film about tribal warfare, he chose to interpret her advice as a statement for the public record rather than a true reflection of her beliefs. When there was a lull in attacks while in the field, he was worried at the prospect that the fighting might cease altogether. He was annoyed at missionaries and government officials in the area who seemed set on putting an end to the fighting, and he explicitly wanted to keep the police and army out of the area during the period of filming, as these law enforcers might have had a restraining effect on "normal" tribal behavior. Missionaries in the area seemed to feel that if the filmmakers were not actively trying to stop the killing, they were implicitly condoning and hence promoting it.

Gardner, however, believed that the Dani derived their whole sense of manhood from these war exercises. As he wrote in a 1961 journal entry, "That there is ritual war in the Baliem Valley is something all people who have lived in that valley know for a certainty; but what no one has bothered to find out is what warfare means to those who make it or what it could mean to deprive them of it." As a filmmaker, too, he was attracted to the "extraordinary theatricality and raw energy" of this "spectacle" of "300–500 decorated and armed warriors dancing against 8,000-foot peaks." And he confesses now that he was also "in the grip of almost obsessive thinking, in which naïveté combined with ambitious goals had me supposing that a film concerned with hand-to-hand violence with ritual purpose could speak in a general way to the understanding of human aggression."

Yet his obsession had its limits. He intervened at one point to save the life of a runaway Wittaia woman whom the Dani were planning to kill. "I could not be witness to such an event, despite what some might think its cinematic value," he wrote in explanation. His ambivalence emerges again in his questioning of whether to document the amputation of young girls' finger joints, a part of the grieving ritual. Clearly sickened and appalled by the practice, he nevertheless wonders if "anyone [has] filmed such an event and, if not, has it some irresistible cinematographic allure?" He decides not to film the amputations, but is later sorely tempted to obtain such footage when producer Joseph E. Levine shows interest in acquiring *Dead Birds* for wide theatrical distribution. Levine, who had made his fortune with cheap Hercules movies shot in Italy, was branching out with classier projects like Jean-Luc Godard's *Contempt*. (When the producer demanded more cheesecake with Brigitte Bardot, Godard famously snorted, "Hasn't he ever seen a film of mine?") and pseudo-anthropological exploitation pictures like *The Sky Above, The Mud Below*. Gardner, who can hardly be blamed for thinking that his film might have a chance for much wider circulation if backed by Levine, wrote Heider, still in the field, to ask if it might be possible to film a joint-amputation ritual. But when Levine demanded a total remake of the film, Gardner breathed a sigh of relief and wrote Heider to forget about it, reasoning that showing girls and women with mutilated hands was as effective as presenting the grisly ceremony onscreen.

Gardner himself continually questions, in this book and others, the what and why of his actions as a filmmaker, in a Montaigne-esque methodology of self-examination. Exquisitely sensitive to all of documentary film's ethical risks, he is also brutally honest about the degree to which he may have overstepped the line. By temperament a worrier, with a puritanical Yankee conscience, he seems immune to complacency. It may be truest to say that what intrigues him most is the problematic, impure, and unresolved nature of experience: the impossibility of avoiding "dirty hands."

I have known Gardner for over thirty years. What strikes me most about him is the contrast between his tremendous competence and his profound self-doubt. Blessed with movie-star good looks, a privileged background, and an inherited social ease, he also betrays at times a surprisingly fragile and vulnerable emotional make-up. He cannot be said to lack confidence or ego, but he is a modest man, especially respectful of other artists. There is also a streak of solemn sadness in him, which he readily acknowledges.

In 2006 I interviewed Gardner in front of an audience at the New York Public Library's Donnell Media Center. In answer to a question about why he identified with marginalized cultures, he said, "I think I was born a melancholy person, and it was not difficult for me to see that film was a melancholy way of looking at the world. If I stayed at home, I might not find enough melancholy or be able to express the kinds of melancholy I thought I could in an environment or culture I was less familiar with."

Asked why he thought film was intrinsically melancholic, he said, "Film incarnates death for me, because when I see a film, particularly actuality film, or when I look at the wonderful renderings of humanity by the great photographers of the world, it seems to me that in those images is the story we can tell without knowing what the whole story is—but know that it will surely end in death."

Death plays a key role in *Dead Birds*. But above and beyond the bloodshed, the film poses a philosophical question: What effect does a man's knowing he is mortal have on the conduct of his life? Gardner, who has often said he used anthropology as an instrument of self-discovery, never specifies in the pages of this book which personal threads of suppressed aggression or internal anger might have linked him to his bloodthirsty material. Perhaps a temperamental pessimism drew him to the subject of ritual war. I would suggest, however, that in the end the film has less to do with killing than with mourning.

There is a specific way in which the making of *Dead Birds* connects to death: the tragic fate of soundman and photographer Michael Rockefeller. Young, talented, and idealistic, Rockefeller died shortly after the film was shot, while on a quite separate trip to collect indigenous art in another part of New Guinea. The simultaneity of his death with the final stage of editing the film seems to haunt Gardner's recollections of making *Dead Birds*, and the shadow cast on the film by Rockefeller's death has been lasting and profound. In one of the more hair-raising admissions recorded in these pages, Gardner says he hushed up the fact that "Michael was grazed by an arrow in battle" to keep the authorities from stopping the film project. Might some element of guilt or remorse for exposing his companions to danger have found expression in Gardner's anguish when Rockefeller disappeared off the coast of New Guinea? The story of Michael Rockefeller's death and of Gardner's own journey to New Guinea with Michael's father, Governor Nelson Rockefeller, in an attempt to get to the bottom of the tragedy, is one of the most touching parts of this book.

In the more than forty years since it was first shown, *Dead Birds* has been regularly screened at conferences and film festivals, shown in classrooms and on television, released on videotape and again on DVD, and acknowledged as one of the classics of ethnographic cinema.

As it happens, ethnographic cinema is a problematic field, fraught with intellectual and ethical dilemmas, and some degree of guilt inevitably accompanies the suggestion of colonialist exploitation in the filming of indigenous people. Filmmakers risk being unable to satisfy the often contradictory demands of anthropology as science and cinema. They face the danger of sentimentalizing or patronizing the group being studied by overemphasizing the exotic or folkloric elements of a culture. They may insufficiently register cultural change in order to present a romantic picture of the "primitive." They may be tempted to distort reality—or accused of having done so—by staging reenactments or instigating events, or by scrambling chronologies and spatial contexts through editing. They may alter a group's behavior by the camera's presence, or introduce objects and technologies from the developed world that destabilize traditional cultures and economies. They may intervene inappropriately in rituals, or not intervene when to do nothing borders on the immoral. Guilt comes with the territory of documentary and ethnographic cinema.

Ever since Luis Buñuel's dispassionate filming of the killing of a donkey in *Land Without Bread,* the ethics of documentary filmmakers have been questioned and examined. Critics often make the point that almost all anti-war movies are secretly pro-war movies, glorifying violence by showing the excitement of battle. Seen in this light, *Dead Birds* is also not exactly pacifist: it exalts the skill in hand-to-hand combat and the cunning necessary to take another person's life. But does that make it immoral or untrue? Shuddering at "the sudden and pointless bloodiness of the affair," after witnessing a battle, Gardner nevertheless asked, in a journal entry, " I even wonder if it may not be true, that to take a life is the most intense, possibly ultimate, human experience there is."

Since *Dead Birds* was first shown, the field of ethnographic cinema has developed stricter guidelines, as Karl Heider—who had been part of the original expedition—has articulated in his standard text on visual anthropology, *Ethnographic Film.* For instance, it is desirable that whole acts and whole persons be presented whenever possible, that close-ups be avoided, that the filmmaker's presence be reflexively acknowledged, and that the film be backed up by written ethnographic material that explains and analyzes the visual record. Heider, noting that in many ways *Dead Birds* satisfied these criteria of ethnographic "truth," also pointed out that "the battle sequences in *Dead Birds* combined footage shot at different battles," and that "even though Robert Gardner filmed most of the battle scenes in *Dead Birds* with normal focal-length lenses, they had the effect of foreshortening the scene, and so the front lines appear to be much closer to each other than they actually were."

Another inevitable "distortion" was the use of so-called wild sound. Lightweight synchronous sound equipment was not available, and audio recorded by Michael Rockefeller without the camera's presence was added to the images in editing. Unlike today's digital video filmmakers, Gardner could not see the raw footage while on location, and we learn from these pages that much of Gardner's anxiety in the field came from shooting "blind," never knowing if there was a light leak in a camera magazine, if exposures were correct, or if the developing labs back home would damage the negatives.

There were other hardships faced by the crew in New Guinea: a brutal sun, almost impassable swamps, copious flies, drenching rain, dysentery, sand fly fever, humidity so intense it caused the film stock to swell and the camera to jam, hostile officials, stray arrows, and native children who kicked the tripod—not to mention loneliness, boredom, and fear of failure. Werner Herzog has said that "humiliation and strain are essential parts of filmmaking," and Gardner would appear to share with Herzog the premise of moviemaking as a self-imposed ordeal. There were missed opportunities, as happens to any documentary maker, such as having to change film magazines while a dead boy's body was being carried to its funeral pyre. But there were also hunches that paid off and sudden improbable pieces of luck, like finding in the nearby home of a Massachusetts collector the very cowrie shells Gardner needed to buy the goodwill of the Dani.

Gardner has had half a lifetime to play back in his mind the moves, the miracles, the triumphs, and regrets of that first, heroic adventure that launched him on his filmmaking journey. This book is the result of that reflection.

One final bit of second-guessing on the filmmaker's part ought to be addressed: his worry about placing "the burden of language" on *Dead Birds* through its voice-over narration. Gardner says in these pages that he has considered going back to "rewrite the narration, which I have often thought too heavy and occasionally arch." He may also be responding to the fact that some anthropologists have criticized his soundtrack, which describes the thoughts and feelings of the Dani protagonists. I have no problem with this storytelling stratagem, and think that spoken words belong in motion pictures as much as images. I disagree fundamentally with the viewpoint put forward by Heider, for instance, that narration in ethnographic cinema is a "cinematically weak" device that draws our attention away from the immediacy of the images and actions.

Gardner's retrospective questioning of the narration of *Dead Birds* may also reflect his own evolution as a documentary filmmaker, as he developed a preference for wordless images without voice-over commentary or dialogue. He uses this approach most spectacularly in his other masterpiece, *Forest of Bliss*. But *Forest of Bliss* shows Hindus preparing corpses in Benares, India, a practice that would be readily understood by most Western viewers. Very few of us could have known what was going on with *Dead Birds'* New Guinea tribesmen unless we were given some guiding commentary.

The memorable narration in *Dead Birds* provides much more than contextual information, however. Superbly delivered in Gardner's grave, melancholy voice, it supplies the film's philosophical and poetic dimensions and sets its quintessentially mournful tone. It crystallizes and unites the images. I find a generosity in the filmmaker's attempt to put into his own eloquent words the significance of the events we have been allowed to witness. In this respect, *Dead Birds* is not only a classic of ethnographic cinema, but a bridge to the essay film, that rare, tricky subgenre in which the filmmaker courageously tells us what he or she is thinking. We learn much about the Dani from the narration of *Dead Birds*, but we also learn about the nature of Gardner's personal preoccupations in making the film, and come to understand why he feels so strongly that, for him, anthropology was a voyage to the self. A part of that voyage is chronicled here, in *Making* Dead Birds: *Chronicle of a Film.*

Weyak gazing at the frontier

introduction

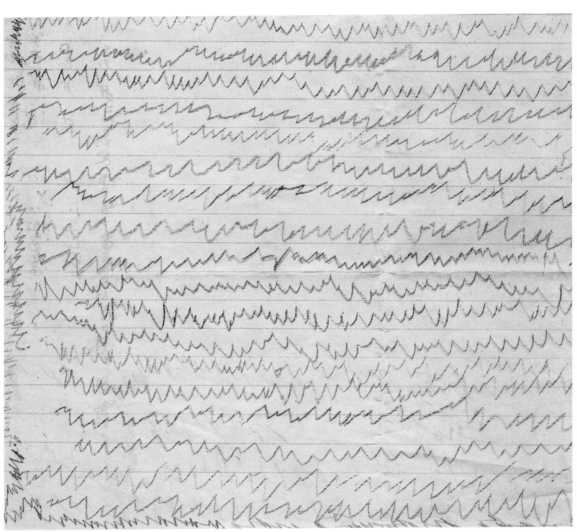

A letter sent to Gardner from Wali, February 1962

Almost ten years ago, when I had abandoned my teaching and admin-
istrative life at Harvard, I made the decision to put this book together. It
happened when I was doing some housekeeping so necessary in my pro-
fession of filmmaking. While I was reviewing, sorting, and identifying
miles of motion pictures accumulated over nearly half a century, the question occurred of how certain parts of that long trail of imagery and the
paper documents engendered in its creation had come into being. What
was it that provoked or compelled me to go down particular paths in
search of particular cinematic ends, especially given the range of possibilities the world offers as a stage upon which humans play? This was a question I not only asked myself, but one others have frequently asked me in
the course of many years.

It was to seek answers to these and other questions that I resurrected
letters, cables, lists, logs, journals, and other even more obscure sources.
More specifically, I began to look for my reasons for choosing to make the
film *Dead Birds* and for the tendencies of mind that determined the way
it was made and the shape it ultimately took. In short, I wanted to see if
I could possibly demonstrate by reference to this heap of documentation
that there was purpose and reason in my effort to employ the art of
film to a humane observation of a remote and seemingly alien group
of people.

The story of this film starts in the years just before I left the American
West to start graduate work in anthropology. My short life on the West
Coast began in Los Angeles as a semi-aspiring or aspiring semi-actor and
continued briefly in Seattle as a novice filmmaker. During this interval my
fate was to read and be so taken by Ruth Benedict's *Patterns of Culture*
that filmmaking urges quite overcame all reasonable hesitations, and I
resolved to bring a camera to a surviving community of the Kwakiutl
nation she had so compellingly described in her book.

Owing to a set of curious coincidences, I also at this time managed
to fall in with Sidney Peterson, a member of the San Francisco avant-garde
film community who happened to be the husband of the sister of the wife
of my dentist. Peterson had aspirations similar to my own and almost the
same lack of technical competence, despite having made a few intensely
personal and much admired experimental films. Not surprisingly, our
dreams of making a narrative feature of the rise and fall of the magnificent Kwakiutl were never realized. The film was to have told the story of
the daughter of a Kwakiutl chief who was in love with a traveling salesman. This salesman was a real person of Canadian citizenship whom I
met in Seattle, where he promoted excursions to Fort Rupert, British
Columbia, to visit an "authentic" Kwakiutl chief presiding over a remnant
Kwakiutl village.

All that came from that period of my apprenticeship in film were
three small works, two about impoverished and declining Kwakiutl living

Gardner and Sidney Peterson, 1950

in Blunden Harbour, B.C., and one about the painter Mark Tobey, who was living in Seattle. For all of them I undertook the editing, writing, and direction, but only with the one about Tobey did I begin what would become a long involvement with image making. These films still exist in the obscurity most such efforts nowadays enjoy. But the two primitive shorts about the Kwakiutl turn out to have been nearly all that was ever done, other than *In the Land of Head-Hunters*, Edward Curtis's elaborate and mostly invented 1914 account of Northwest Coast native life, to put this extraordinary people on film in a realistic manner. The Mark Tobey film was selected by the Venice Film Festival in the summer of 1952, the year it was made, and these days it is occasionally shown to pay tribute to an important American artist at mid-career.

It was at this juncture that concerns about my future caused me to seize upon the idea of getting more education. I may have wanted the respectability I lacked as the result of my failed efforts in an industry in what was then and may still be the low repute of cinema. I was unseen as an actor, and nearly unwatched as a filmmaker.

My choice of locale was where I had been an undergraduate, the familiar and serious-minded East, not the trendier West. In this I was obeying a dictum of Mark Tobey's about the East being a crucifixion of the body and the West of the mind. I had had enough of the great outdoors, and so I moved to Cambridge, Massachusetts, in September 1952.

I was married and we had a one-year-old son, which meant I was older and presumably more experienced than most of the others who were entering graduate school with me. Had I looked carefully at this cohort, I would have seen that they had preoccupations quite different from my own. In 1952 there was an unmistakable odor of scientism in the September air, which seemed to mesmerize my fellow students. The Iron Curtain had been rung down and the Cold War was on, so it was a time when knowledge was being optimistically applied to the perceived needs of keeping an uneasy peace. I was at first comforted, and even experienced a few faint illusions of purpose as a budding scholar. Might I, too, become a kind of physician looking after a sick society? Anthropology was widely thought to be a road to understanding, even ameliorating, such troubling issues as racism and injustice, not to speak of violence and war. It could do this because it was thought to be objective. Humanistic tendencies, on the other hand, were considered soft and were embraced only by an embattled minority. The pursuit of prediction and similar ways of arriving at certainties was just much more appealing. Such, at least, was the prevailing mood those days and, from the start, I struggled to fall in line.

Happily there were figures such as Clyde Kluckhohn, my professor at Harvard, who had written *Mirror for Man* (betokening my eventual interest in devices like cameras?), and Claude Lévi-Strauss, who had just written *Tristes Tropiques* (betokening my obsession about the essential melancholy

4

of life?). They and a number of others kept hope alive for an anthropology that welcomed intuitive, even subjective, casts of mind. Also available to the cause of humanism were the words of writers like Charles Doughty in *Travels in Arabia Deserta,* Robert Graves in *The White Goddess,* and Charles Darwin in *The Voyage of the Beagle.* Books like these, though not assigned in class, were never out of reach. Of wider currency in those days was psychoanalysis, thought by some to be a key to comprehending human behavior, even if Freud's writing inconveniently blurred the boundaries between philosophy, art, and science. I even came to view his *Psychopathology of Everyday Life* as a masterful treatment for a nonfiction film, with its lucid writing about the inner and outer lives of human beings at the margins of society. For me, pursuing such matters was one of anthropology's truest callings.

A few anthropologists were known to think psychoanalysis was a desirable part of one's methodological arsenal. Margaret Mead was an exception. She answered my question of whether she had been analyzed by saying she did not need to have been because she worked so much with children. She might have been right. In any case, what might psychoanalysis mean to the story in this book? My answer is that its emphasis on self-comprehension guided me into thinking there could be an anthropology that revealed the meaning of one's own life as well as, or even better than, the meaning of the lives of "others." I thought I saw in psychoanalysis a companion doctrine to Clyde Kluckhohn's, the idea of a mirror that could be held up not only to Man, but also to our individual selves. By the end of my career as a graduate student in 1956, I was sure that whatever film I might make about the world outside myself would have to be done with mirrors (as is virtually inevitable in the case of cameras) that also revealed me and my inner world.

The company I kept during the mid-fifties in Cambridge must also have played a role in the development of my filmmaking proclivities and thus in the larger story about *Dead Birds,* including not only the decision to go to New Guinea but the way I filmed there and how I later shaped that work. By reason of both chance and circumstance, many of the people I saw most frequently, aside from graduate school comrades and teachers, were artists and writers, especially poets. In Seattle I had come to be a friend of Theodore Roethke, at that time a teacher of English at the University of Washington. It was he who opened the doors for me of his fellow poets in New England, like Donald Hall and Robert Lowell, and in due course Ted Hughes, with whom I would work in the late sixties on a script for a feature film based on Alan Moorehead's *Cooper's Creek.* Another poet, Stanley Kunitz, was living in Cambridge for a spell and came from time to time to a workshop I gave in the Peabody Museum in the late fifties about films and their making. I remember him telling us he had gotten most of his early childhood education watching two or three movies a day with his mother in Worcester, Massachusetts.

I ought also to mention the Poet's Theatre, an impassioned group of writers, actors, and other artists and lovers of the arts. It was the creation of Mary Manning, wife of a law professor and intimate in her youth of Samuel Beckett and W. B. Yeats. William Alfred, who professed Old English at Harvard, wrote plays in verse that were performed on the Poet's Theatre stage, and stately figures like Edith Sitwell, Archibald MacLeish, and E. E. Cummings came and went reading their work on a regular basis. It was a time when I was captivated as much by words as imagery, which clearly explains, for me at least, the burden of language I placed on *Dead Birds* in the form of narration.

In those days little was happening locally regarding the practice or study of cinema other than a few college film societies (at Harvard it was Ivy Films), most of which were devoted to narrative features. In New York the groundbreaking model for alternative or independent work, Cinema 16, was flourishing, and Frances Flaherty was in Brattleboro, Vermont, eloquently evangelizing her husband Robert's legacy. In any event, it was to the "documentary" that I was most drawn, and though Flaherty's *Nanook* was thought to be the "ur" film documentary, I preferred his *Man of Aran,* which I had first come upon in Seattle at a film society showing. That was when I saw other arresting work such as Maya Deren's *Study in Choreography for Camera,* or *Pas de Deux,* Vittorio De Sica's *Bicycle Thieves,* Roberto Rossellini's *Open City,* Georges Franju's *Blood of the Beasts,* and Jean Vigo's *A Propos de Nice,* to mention a few of many. Each of these films gave me what Samuel Johnson called the repose resulting from "the stability of truth," and I was ensnared by their charms as works of art.

In the Harvard film culture of 1952 I knew of only two quite novel undertakings: ultra-high-speed 16mm-film documentation of bat behavior in the Biology Department, sponsored by the U.S. Navy, and visual recording through one-way glass of students participating in experiments using hallucinogens, run by Timothy Leary in the Psychology Department. My own efforts did not bear fruit until 1956, when *The Hunters* was completed in the basement of the Peabody Museum, and early 1957, when the Film Study Center was officially founded.

Throughout the fifties, John Otis (Jo) Brew was director of the Peabody Museum and an advisor to Lawrence Marshall of Cambridge, a retired businessman who sponsored a series of trips to the Kalahari Desert by his talented family. At Brew's suggestion, I was asked in 1955 to help Marshall's son John, who was still an undergraduate, to review the available footage and develop a longer film from an existing 45-minute version of what would become *The Hunters.* Eventually the film grew to more than 70 minutes and, when it was publicly released, quickly began to enjoy wider than usual attention as a nearly feature-length nonfiction

J. O. Brew and Gardner

account of a small, delicate, and vivid hunting-and-gathering society in the Kalahari Desert of southwest Africa. Unfortunately, it was not until after *The Hunters* was completed that I was able, in 1957, to join John for a period of filming among the Bushmen.

Later on, *The Hunters'* principal and talented young author started graduate school at Yale, while I set about establishing the Film Study Center as a small, visually minded production and research unit in the Peabody. I began by thinking of sequels to *The Hunters* that might be made from the vast accumulation of footage shot mostly by John over a period of several years beginning around 1950.

Following the editing of some preliminary film continuities, it was decided in late 1959 or early 1960 to put everything into John's hands when he left Yale and came home to Cambridge. He was the person who, with his writer sister Elizabeth Marshall and his ethnographer mother Lorna Marshall, knew most about the Bushmen, and he was utterly devoted to them. To aid him in his endeavors, and with the help of Margaret Mead, I found Timothy Asch, who was later to accumulate important footage of his own about the Yanomamo of Venezuela. Theirs became a co-worker relationship that lasted many years, and which immediately permitted me to go about finding my own next film.

John Marshall and Gardner

The account of that process, which occupies the pages ahead, has been drawn from various and sundry letters and notebooks and a miscellany of other documents. Where these sources appear to need clarification or amplification, I have taken the liberty of inserting my own voice even at this lengthy temporal remove. Of course, there are lapses in my long-term memory, and so questions, even minor mysteries, remain. But none, I trust, that prevent the reader from being told a detailed and reliable story of the finding, making, and finally more or less abandoning to whatever posterity it deserves the film *Dead Birds*.

Before turning to that story, something should be said about the main figures, the characters, as it were, and about the situation of the world we were headed into.

I was contacted in 1959 by Harold Coolidge, a distant cousin who was running the Pacific Science Board in Washington, D.C., and who knew I was casting about for a major project. He told me of an obscure New Guinea tribe that was making ritual war. It was not long before I was entertaining the idea of making a film in what was then called Netherlands New Guinea (NNG), which made up one half of the world's second largest island. At the time, the Dutch were committed to releasing this possession from their governance but had not yet found a suitable political arrangement for independence. The story of how this vast territory of countless independent languages and cultures became fraught with the politics of not only the Third but also the First and Second Worlds requires its own book. Here I will only note that the United States would play a prominent role in terms not only of geopolitics but of rampant capitalism. What I knew of these matters by the time I returned from filming in New Guinea was enough to have me urge McGeorge Bundy, former dean of the faculty at Harvard who had since become President Kennedy's national security advisor, not to purchase rapport with Sukarno's Indonesia by using New Guinea as a hostage to fortune. But this attempt availed little, as did a series of op-ed pieces I wrote for the *Boston Globe* on the subject. It must be said that when I originally prepared to go to New Guinea, I thought mainly of how I could carefully document a small part of the still accessible and fully functioning indigenous life, which was then under the protection and care of Dr. Victor de Bruyn, the head of Native Affairs in that troubled territory.

De Bruyn was a trained fieldworker and an experienced observer who had spent many months watching the Japanese make war through-out the South Pacific. The title of his biography by Lloyd Rhys, *Jungle Pimpernel,* aptly describes his role throughout World War II. It would be with de Bruyn that I would make all the key decisions regarding where and how I wanted to see the filming enterprise go forward. Two other Dutchmen, Adrian Gerbrands and Jan Broekhuyse, would help in impor-tant ways. Jan was already in NNG serving as a district officer in the valley to which I was hoping to go. He was eventually detached from his official duties and given leave to act as a translator and valued partner in all our undertakings. Gerbrands was a well-known anthropologist who would show me the art of the Asmat on the South Coast of New Guinea and who had helpful friends of all kinds throughout NNG.

From the start, my central purpose was to make a long and ambitious film, and for a time I considered putting together a group of people skilled in the crafts required for such an effort. At the same time, I felt strongly that the filmmaking should be accompanied by other kinds of observa-tion, which tempted me to think of people whom I knew and cared to be with and who could also contribute in as many interesting ways as possi-ble. At one time I had in mind not only still photographers but also writers and even painters. Eventually I was able to enlist Peter Matthiessen, whom I knew for his dry humor as well as for being a gifted writer and skilled naturalist. I remember that I introduced him to the idea of going to NNG at a Sunday lunch party on Martha's Vineyard. (Peter has recently told me I am wrong in thinking that Jane Goodall had come to the party with a baby chimp peeking out of her blouse.)

In the fall of 1961, Michael Rockefeller, a senior at Harvard, sought me out on the recommendation of his roommate, Samuel Putnam. Sam had come to me earlier for advice on a visual project and was soon fascinated by the work we were doing with the Bushmen films. Michael appeared to possess no credentials beyond his modesty and an endless curiosity about a wider world, and especially about preliterate art. I knew nothing of his skill as a photographer, so I challenged him to learn sound recording if he wanted to go to New Guinea. Eliot Elisofon, a well-known color photographer for *Life Magazine,* was a friend through mutual interests in cinema, art, and photography. He was interested in coming for a brief visit, and did so with fine results.

Another responsibility I felt with some urgency concerned the manner in which we undertook the close study of the lives of those we would be filming, recording, writing about, and photographing. All these activities needed to intersect with anthropology, a discipline practiced according to tendencies situated along a continuum from humanistic, where I located myself, to scientific, but always requiring participation in and inquiry into such basic cultural issues as language, social relations, religion, and salient values. Any one of these topics is a tall order, and that is why someone willing to spend not months but years in their study was needed. The person who came and who stayed more than two years was Karl Heider, at that time a graduate student in anthropology at Harvard, with whom I shared an addiction to tobacco and whom I came to know on the steps of the Peabody Museum, where smoking was permitted. Such then was the "team" I assembled. A few others came for a few days at a time, including the botanist Chris Versteegh—I always wanted to know what actually grew in the landscape—and, for a longer period, Sam Putnam, who did significant photography, often in tandem with Michael Rockefeller.

The reason for going to the considerable trouble that finding and making this film required had its origin in an immodest hope that the film might persuade viewers that the people in it are not so different from themselves and that the central concerns of the film, human violence and mortality, are as important to everybody as to the people in the film. In the end, I hope this account can give comfort to those who might follow our example of living in another world, in our case in the midst of neolithic warrior-farmers, and find for themselves an equally informing and arresting time and place to reflect upon in images and words. I continue to think the day has come when it is necessary to learn from the lessons of each other's experiences.

Peter Matthiessen, Gardner, and Karl Heider

The Grand Valley of the Baliem

early thinking

When I walked away from watching Dead Birds
I almost seemed to stagger inside myself. Today I am
still jarred by it and still trying to understand the guilty
significance of what it tells us about ourselves.
—Robert Lowell

January 27, 1959

Harold Coolidge, Pacific Science Board, National Research Council, Washington, D.C., to Robert Gardner (RG), in Cambridge, Massachusetts
The purpose of this letter is to call to your attention the fascinating report which has just been brought out in the *Yale Publications on Anthropology* #54, in which Leopold Pospisil describes the Kapauku Papuans with whom he lived in Netherlands New Guinea. I understand that he is returning to New Guinea, and I find myself wishing that you, or someone with the kind of knowledge of film technology which you have developed, might accompany him and make a parallel record of primitive Papuans to the one that has been made of Kalahari Bushmen. Pospisil, with very limited funds, has made a film of a war between two stone-age villages which is a unique anthropological record.

January 29, 1959

RG to Coolidge

I am very interested in the information you give me about Pospisil. I met him about two years ago just after he had returned from New Guinea and saw his war film. It was a valiant effort and is no doubt a valuable document, but there were so many things wrong with it technically that it can never become a film. I don't mean he didn't approach his subject with feeling and knowledge, I mean he used a camera as if it were a flashlight, pointing it in every direction at once, going at the wrong speed, filming subjects at the wrong distance, most everything scrambled and out of focus. It is one of countless instances of a totally unprepared person taking it upon himself to do a complex piece of work.

As far as the Film Study Center is concerned, New Guinea is of large interest, but because we are hardly able to continue with our work on the Bushmen for want of funds, it is out of the question to now embark on another project. If only some agency somewhere could be sufficiently inspired to realize competent taking of motion pictures is the only means left for preserving an historical record of vast areas of human culture, such demurrers as mine regarding the Papuans would not be necessary. The inspiration will come, of course, when most of the indigenous world has been dumped into the pot of a common technological civilization.

The rapidity with which I answered Coolidge's letter about ritual war among the Kapauku is an indication of my eagerness to be alert to film possibilities. I did not know much about Pospisil or about his work, but I was certainly ready to learn more. Coolidge's reply to my note convinced me of his own enthusiasm.

February 2, 1959

Coolidge to RG

I wanted to have you talk with Dr. de Bruyn about the work you are doing in anthropological films at Harvard. Do you think it would be possible for you and Jo Brew to stay over on Friday, the 27th, when de Bruyn will be coming to Washington so that you can have a good talk with him? It might well be that the Netherlands Government would be willing to finance the expenses that would be involved in your making an anthropological film of some of the remote Papuan peoples using the techniques you have developed for the African Bushmen. The key man in this whole picture would be de Bruyn, and I could give the proposal for such a film my support.

I remember clearly the meeting with de Bruyn. It was at the Cosmos Club, where, as I remember, J. O. Brew was staying. It was my first encounter with de Bruyn, and I recall his quietly intense demeanor. I was also aware of a profound concern he felt for the present—and even more for the future— welfare of the indigenous people in what was then called Netherlands New Guinea. De Bruyn struck me as much more Asian than European in manner. The meeting gave the two of us the opportunity to agree, without saying much at all, on trying to make a collaboration between the Film Study Center and his government.

March 18, 1959

Coolidge to RG

A letter from Victor de Bruyn has just come in from The Hague, in which he says, "This week I will be at the Department of Overseas Affairs in The Hague, where I will also discuss the possibilities of making scientific anthropological pictures of New Guinea tribes as we discussed it at the luncheon at the Cosmos Club. I would appreciate it if you or Professor Brew could send me more detailed information about the Harvard Film Unit of John Marshall and Robert Gardner. In the first place I would like to know what costs are involved in making such pictures. We can figure out the cost of traveling and accommodation in the territory itself..."

By this time the possibility of my making a film in New Guinea was beginning to seem likely. Although I was trying to carry on with the editing of the Marshalls' Bushmen material, I was doing so with difficulty, owing in part to the absence of John, who was at Yale testing the graduate school waters in anthropology. At a certain point it became obvious to me that were I to continue having a major role in what we called the Bushmen Project, I should tell John what was on my mind. Hence my letter of November 5, 1959.

November 5, 1959

RG to John Marshall

What follows amounts to the essentials of my thinking in relation to those as yet undone films which had, by agreement, been assigned to my charge. Until I joined you in Africa, I was, of course, able to see the !Kung only, and quite literally, through your eyes. All my thinking on "The Gatherers" [a sequel to *The Hunters* to be undertaken by Gardner] and the other films was tied indissolubly to the effect on me of the photography you had done. When I came to the Kalahari there were, as you can perhaps imagine, a number of rather violent shocks for which my formal knowledge and vicarious experience of the Bushmen had not prepared me. I recognize that all I had to inform me, beyond the acquaintance I have already described, was intuition. In any case, I became engrossed in what I shall call, for want of a better term, the "despair" of these people. As I have told you, my interest is focused on the Bushmen in their decline, in their death struggles, which I see as a sign both of demise and, perhaps, rebirth. The struggle in death is also the pang of new life.

In my fascination I seized, somewhat ghoulishly, upon our dear Old Lady. She gave me contact, if only in my mind's eye, with the peace and serenity these people may once have had. "The Gatherers" began, in earnest, as I sat by her side and tried so unsuccessfully to see into her with my camera's eye. The object (the Old Lady) which I grew to love, grew itself into the central figure of a film which would portray the life of a !Kung woman, this woman, *all gatherers.*

"The Rhythms"—This film is the most speculative of all that I have pondered. The notion grew from a more formal reaction than in my feelings toward "The Gatherers." Seeing all the film of the Bushmen is like watching a gigantic dance, a vast ballet, if one can compress the product of the senses, that can be apprehended as beats and intervals of gesture and movement. The ordinary tempo of behavior with its variations between individuals is at a deeper layer, where there is a sharing of accomplishment. It is a form of knowing and a form of communion. It is, perhaps, how one Bushman can trust or know, or not trust or know, another. It is how one Bushman knows he is, or is not, loved. As I envisage "The Rhythms," what I would aim for would be a kind of human and actual animation, a series of linked and woven sequences, all echoing each other. Obviously such a film would be valuable less as an exposition of culture than as a study in cinema, one of the aims of the Film Study Center, if nothing else. Yet, still, the possibility remains that with sufficiently keen awareness of the salient and significant physical motions of the !Kung, there would result, in a film such as I am describing, a visual exercise which could impart concentrates or precipitates of social existence. At any rate, the conception is highly cinematic, and its elements are those more of art than what is characteristically the case with documentary filmmaking.

The Old Lady, 1958

And so it is with my thoughts at this point. As you are aware, the films I describe are still ideas and will, no doubt, change with time. Even so, I wanted you to know them now so that with change or without it, there will be a base upon which something can be built.

John Marshall responded to this letter with what I would call now a mixture of concern and irritation. The concern was that I, perhaps anyone, would have the temerity to interpret people and a culture that he knew better than any outsider. He was right in a way. My way of seeing and conceiving films about these people and their culture would be far less authoritative than what he himself could do. His irritation was also understandable, in that he would most probably have to abandon graduate school and resume his work as an editor of what was largely his own work. In fact, it was not long before John did return to Cambridge and to his editing.

During John's absence I continued to edit two or three films we had agreed I should take on. One was of a young couple whose first child died almost as soon as it was born. The father was a musician who, upon the death of his child, threw his instrument, a one-string violin, into the night and left with the child's mother on a long journey. I called the film The Divided Bow. *It was never released.*

Other than editing, I recall feeling sufficient certainty about New Guinea that I set about discovering what I could concerning that island, especially the western highlands. My informal seminar in filmmaking was active, and at least one magical little film, Orange and Blue *by Peter Chermayeff, was finished and widely shown, as sometimes happened in those days with 16mm shorts.*

February 8, 1960

Coolidge to RG

I have just had a note from my friend Victor de Bruyn, written in Netherlands New Guinea, who is extremely anxious to establish close working relationships with anthropologists in this country. He has informed me privately that his government is interested in the Harvard Film Study Center which you told him about, and that under the 1960 territorial budget there is about $6500 reserved as a grant to the Film Study Center for making a film in Netherlands New Guinea.

On getting this letter I was satisfied that undertaking a New Guinea film project was all but certain. The question was only when and how. I began to seek professional encouragement and whatever might be given me in the way of blessings, as my notes on two encounters with prominent figures on the cultural scene record:

15

February 9, 1960

RG memorandum of conversation in New York with Robert Goldwater of the Museum of Primitive Art

Goldwater was in the midst of museum affairs when I went to see him. Various agents, peddlers, and officials were underfoot everywhere. Nevertheless, he seemed both willing and anxious to talk about film and primitive art. He said he supposed we were between ten and fifty years too late, but he quickly qualified this by saying he had no firsthand knowledge of the situation as it stood now in the most promising areas. The areas he thought most likely for documentary coverage of art, religion, and social life were in Melanesia and isolated parts of West Africa. He spoke of New Guinea, New Hebrides, and New Britain.

February 9, 1960

RG memorandum of conversation with Margaret Mead in New York

When the notion of doing [a] film study of a ritually and artistically alive primitive group was raised, Mead showed immediate enthusiasm. I mentioned Goldwater's caution about it being too late, and she felt no sympathy for that. The areas she suggested were the same as Goldwater with one or two more specific additions. She also suggested that a "reactive" group be chosen. That is to say, one that has reacted against the western influence it has had enough time to observe, feel, and then reject. She pointed out that there are big problems working in places such as New Guinea. First, the population is composed of small groups. Second, these groups are scattered. And third, the chance of working with them depends on the good relations one makes with key individuals in the groups involved. Should one of these people die or leave or an epidemic hit the whole group, the working arrangement which one had could change overnight.

Margaret Mead and her interpreter, John Kilipak, in Pere Village, 1975

February 12, 1960

RG to Coolidge

I am delighted that de Bruyn has not forgotten us. Indeed he seems to have kept a careful eye out for us. New Guinea has been very much on our minds recently inasmuch as another project is definitely desirable, though the destination is still uncertain. New Guinea is a possibility for several reasons. First, it is still relatively unmodified in places by western influences. Second, there is a group going from Holland (a friend, Adri Gerbrands, included) to do a study in New Guinea of art and ritual. Third, I have remembered de Bruyn's earlier expressions of interest and cooperative spirit. Perhaps some plans can develop.

I was clearly at the business of fanning the embers of interest on the part of those most likely to make what I wanted to transpire happen. I was not ready to allow anyone off the hook, even though I was perhaps partly playing the reluctant suitor. I had submitted to de Bruyn a budget for the pro-

posed project, and was surprised to subsequently hear from Adrian Gerbrands on the subject. Gerbrands was a scholar, a man who had survived the dangers and hardships of an underground life as a partisan in World War II Holland, but he was not a filmmaker. He belonged to a conservative sodality of academics who thought of film as an interesting adjunct for fieldwork.

February 16, 1960

A. A. Gerbrands, in Holland, to RG

A few days ago I heard that *The Hunters* was awarded a prize in Florence. Congratulations!

Government officials asked my opinion on the budget you made for Victor de Bruyn for a similar project in Dutch New Guinea. To put it quite frankly, I believe your shooting ratio of 10:1 to be rather high. Moreover, I am of the opinion that shooting 100,000 feet in New Guinea in four to six months, as you proposed to de Bruyn, will not yield scientifically reliable material, unless you know really exceedingly well the culture to be filmed.

March 8, 1960

RG to Gerbrands

Greetings after these few years since Prague [UNESCO conference in 1958]. I often recall the pleasant fellowship of those days and especially the stimulation of some of the discussion between the "scientifically" and the "artistically" oriented delegates. There is still no satisfactory resolution of this conflict as far as I am concerned, except to say that it refers to a spurious dichotomy. The more I have thought and worked in this area, the more I am convinced that there is no substitute for competence in the field ("science," if you please) and inspiration in the editing room ("art," if I may be permitted). Without both there can be no significance to the employment of the film medium. One must be both an accurate observer and a sensitive interpreter.

I am interested that your government asked for your opinion on my suggestion to do a film in New Guinea. Let me say that 10:1 is a very average ratio in documentary or ethnographic coverage. With the Bushmen material we will eventually come out with a 100:1 ratio. This means only that one shot in 100 will be used in any of the *edited* films made from the whole corpus, *NOT* that only one shot in 100 was usable. Now when you question the *scientific* reliability of any shooting, you imply that this is a controllable factor. My opinion is that even a so-called scientist-anthropologist staying ten years in New Guinea could easily produce no significant results photographically either in the "scientific" or purely pictorial sense.

My main purpose in the New Guinea project would be to make as complete a photographic survey of a relatively restricted area as possible, preferably the more unexplored areas of the highland interior.

Adrian Gerbrands in the Asmat, 1961

In the six or so weeks preceding the following letter to Michael Rockefeller, he and I had a number of casual meetings in which we talked more and more seriously about the New Guinea venture. Michael wanted almost more than anything to be a part of it, but he had to find a way to feel a real contributor. He was most interested in a role as one of the photographers, but he accepted the necessity of performing duties recording sound for the film I would be making. This letter was meant to set forth some guidelines for his thinking about the task ahead. It was also an effort to explain what it was that he (and I) would be asking Michael's family foundation to help support.

April 20, 1960   **RG to Michael Rockefeller, in Cambridge**

In this letter, I've tried to put down in a summary fashion, first, the offer made to the Film Study Center by the Netherlands Government; second, a brief proposal as to what we, on our part, might do with this offer.

As a result of several reviews, the Netherlands Government has decided to make a concrete offer of assistance, as follows:

1. A cash subsidy for the year 1961–62 in the amount of 25,000 guilders ($6500).
2. The services of an anthropologist (Jan Broekhuyse) currently working for the Dutch Government as a District Officer in the Baliem Valley of the central highlands.
3. Transportation on waterways in the highlands and coastal area of Dutch New Guinea.
4. Interpreters and guides as needed.
5. Police protection for work outside the administrated territory of the highlands.
6. The possibility of getting KLM air transportation at the government rate.
7. The possibility of getting sea cargo rates on Dutch lines at a reduced cost.
8. The full cooperation of the Dutch officials throughout the territory, including the very valuable help, from the moment we arrive, of Dr. Victor de Bruyn, the native advisor.

Speaking for his government and also from his own long personal experience as an anthropologist in New Guinea, Dr. de Bruyn strongly recommended that we choose the Grand Valley of the Baliem River as the place to do our work. From the information he was able to give us in conversation about the topography and demography of this region, it is reasonable to assume that it would be quite feasible for a film team to settle into a fairly large village or hamlet-like cluster and remain for a relatively extended length of time. This would create the opportunity to live in close contact and on increasingly intimate terms with a manageable group of people (under 100). After three or four weeks, assuming that decent rapport can be established, team members should know the natives by name and would be beginning to relate to them as individuals. Documentation can then proceed in a way that presents the natives as actual personalities and not as curiosities.

The first intellectual task will be to develop an understanding of the major cultural themes, as well, of course, as gaining a familiarity with the routine of their daily lives. On the assumption that the field-work would extend over a period of from four to six months, it is possible that by the end of that time most, if not all, salient features of the culture would have come under observation. Inasmuch as the culture of this particular region is not known, one of the responsibilities falling upon anyone going to it for the first time is to report it comprehensively. This, however, would be a primarily literary occupation. Photography, in the time available, cannot hope to make an exhaustive record of an entire culture, and this is not the principal function of photography anyway. The photographic task is more selective. The problem will be to find those areas of behavior which embrace events and situations that best illustrate the main features and characteristics of the culture in question. Every society has focal interests which tend to distinguish them from other social groups. In one group it may be a special emphasis placed on ritual surrounding death, in another a highly developed system of values regarding hunting, in another a sense of importance of all males as warriors. These highly elaborated interests are, in a sense, the main threads holding together whole patterns of social life and therefore they lend themselves, quite appropriately, as themes to describe it. The photographer's responsibility will be to first recognize and then use such themes as threads or continuities. This is at least the procedure. Nothing can be said at this point about what themes will be used.

By the end of April 1960, I was still looking for whatever I could find about the world within and near the Grand Valley of the Baliem. I had started with a search of the photographic records of the American Museum of Natural History Expedition led by Richard Archbold, which in 1945 had revealed the Baliem Valley to western eyes for the first time. From there I had turned to a missionary organization called the Christian and Missionary Alliance (CAMA), hoping to read contemporary eyewitness reports regularly sent home by these Protestant Evangelical missionaries in Netherlands New Guinea to their enthusiastic parishioners in the U.S. Jo Brew made the first formal contact with the organization on our behalf. (It was I who wrote the letter, though Brew signed it to give it more authority.)

The territory of Kurelu

April 27, 1960

**J. O. Brew, Director, Harvard Peabody Museum,
to the Christian and Missionary Alliance, New York**

The Peabody Museum plans to embark on an anthropological study of the Grand Valley of the Baliem River in Netherlands New Guinea in May or June, 1961. One of the main purposes of this project will be to make a thorough record in moving pictures of native life in the Valley while this is still possible. To this end, Mr. Robert Gardner, Director of the Peabody Museum Film Study Center, who is experienced in this sort of work, will be in charge.

Sometime during the first half of May the members of the traveling group will be together in New York, and I expect to be with them. Would you be so kind as to permit us to come to see you and discuss the possibility of our obtaining access to the valuable information you have?

April 27, 1960

Brew to Victor de Bruyn, in New Guinea

Considerable progress has been made since our conference on April 7 in the formulation of our ideas about going to the Grand Valley of the Baliem River. As our plans develop you will be hearing from either Mr. Gardner or myself, I imagine, quite regularly.

We have succeeded already in obtaining enough money [from the Norman Foundation, Rockefeller Foundation, Netherlands New Guinea Government, and Wenner-Gren Foundation] to assure the field season, and we are now beginning to explore the possibilities of financing the subsequent work back here, which will be necessary to produce the moving pictures. You will understand that we shall not embark on the expedition unless we know that we will have sufficient financial support to complete the work upon our return here.

May 12, 1960

RG memorandum of conversations with Leopold Pospisil, Eliot Elisofon, Margaret Mead, and Michael Rockefeller, in New York

Dr. Pospisil has spent a total of fifteen months among the Kapauku Papuans of the Western Highlands in Dutch New Guinea. He was able to give many pieces of practical advice. Because of his training under Nazi tutelage in starvation tactics during the war, Pospisil is an able field man. He believes in the lightest possible supply load, taking for himself only sugar, salt, tea, dry milk, tobacco, and small amounts of tinned meat. The largest part of his diet he procured from the native gardens.

Tuesday night we had dinner with Eliot Elisofon. Eliot's experience in New Guinea was too meager to fit him as a guide or counselor on that subject, but his vast knowledge and experience with photography in the field, including New Guinea, will make him a valuable contact. He made the sensible suggestion that Mike, if he is going in the van to New Guinea, should make some forays into various parts of Papua—the Sepik and Fly—as well as Dutch New Guinea

21

in an attempt to locate and possibly collect some primitive art. This would also provide Mike with a period of shakedown and orientation. Eliot was very anxious to go over the still photographic equipment problems and give advice and instruction to Mike and Sam [Putnam] along this line. Eliot also suggested that he could probably join the expedition for a while on *Life*'s salary, if his fare could be paid. This suggestion seems to me to merit careful consideration.

On May 11 we met with Margaret Mead. She seemed genuinely glad to see another Peabody Film and Anthropology venture underway. She talked mostly of what to expect from Dutch anthropologists and district officials. I think we should try to get a line on Broekhuyse as soon as possible. She claimed that the Dutch were characteristically both cruel and cowardly. De Bruyn is an obvious exception. She thought this might interfere with our relation to any group. She warned of the dangers of the indigenous police boys. According to her, they rape and steal. At the suggestion that we might do some study of warfare she reacted quite violently, intimating that this was irresponsible. Her point was that in photographing or even just observing hostile behavior of this kind, we would be condoning it and thus letting down the administration, "making it unsafe for every white man," as she put it.

I had the feeling at the time of this conversation with Mead that she was making a point in order to be on the record more than because she really felt my plans to focus on the intertribal hostilities in the Baliem Valley were irresponsible. In any case, she was happy a few years later to write the Introduction to a book on the Dani I chose to call Gardens of War.

June 6, 1960

RG to Gerbrands

Because of your very attractive offer to have me as your guest, I have changed my reservations and will be coming directly to Amsterdam. I look forward eagerly to hearing about your plans in New Guinea and telling you of ours.

June 16, 1960

RG to Louis L. King, Christian and Missionary Alliance (CAMA)

I hope I made it clear to you on Tuesday that your cooperation and kind interest in the problems surrounding my New Guinea affairs are deeply appreciated. I think I learned more in the time I was able to spend talking with you and looking at your field workers' reports than I have consulting all the books and specialists so far encountered. With respect to Bromley [Myron Bromley, CAMA missionary and linguist], I am very much counting on an introduction to this man so that we can start on the language.

By the end of June 1960, the trip to New Guinea was being actively organized. Michael was dividing his time between his obligations as a reservist in the U.S. Army and as a key participant in the preparations. I had largely withdrawn from my role in the Bushmen project, which John had by this time come home to and in which he was deeply involved. I served as a member of a faculty committee appointed by Harvard President Nathan Pusey to plan the recently funded Visual Arts Center. These were to be my last months at the Peabody before setting out for New Guinea. During this time an enormous number of pieces of a rather complex puzzle had to be fitted together.

June 24, 1960   **RG to Rockefeller, in New York**

I have thought twice about your going in my stead to Nikon [to arrange donation of several of Nikon's recently introduced 35mm single-lens reflex cameras] and it seems to me now that I had better do as I told Silverman [at Nikon] and go myself. It will be OK for me to run down, maybe with Sam for a day early in July.

I am sending you the book on sound recording, which you must guard from loss as it belongs to a library. I'll get all the other books and transcripts of Christian and Missionary Alliance stuff to you as I gather it together.

June 27, 1960   **RG to Gerbrands**

I think it would be a very sensible thing for me to meet, if only briefly and formally, with some of the officials you mention. I am anxious to have it all well understood why Harvard is sending a group to New Guinea and who will be in it. I have in mind possible difficulties when we send film and other material out. Therefore, I should speak with someone in the customs branch of your government.

I have described in the Introduction the circumstances of my early summer meeting with Peter Matthiessen. The matter of his joining me had come to a rapid resolution, and Peter's participation was a source of comfort to me as I looked ahead. His coming meant that humor would never be absent, no matter how grim the circumstances. Without being convinced of the treacheries awaiting us at the hands of the highlanders of New Guinea luridly described by missionaries, we were all a trifle apprehensive. So Peter's wry outlook concerning such matters and his experience of the world, which was at least as wide as my own, were a distinct comfort.

July 5, 1960   **RG to Peter Matthiessen, on Long Island**

I'll try to put in this letter some of the backlog of information and ideas that have accumulated since our talk.

I have enclosed several things. One is an extremely crude map of the Baliem (Grand) Valley area. As I told you, this valley is approximately forty miles long by twenty miles wide. You can get a vague feeling for it by looking at the *National Geographic*, vol. LXXIX,

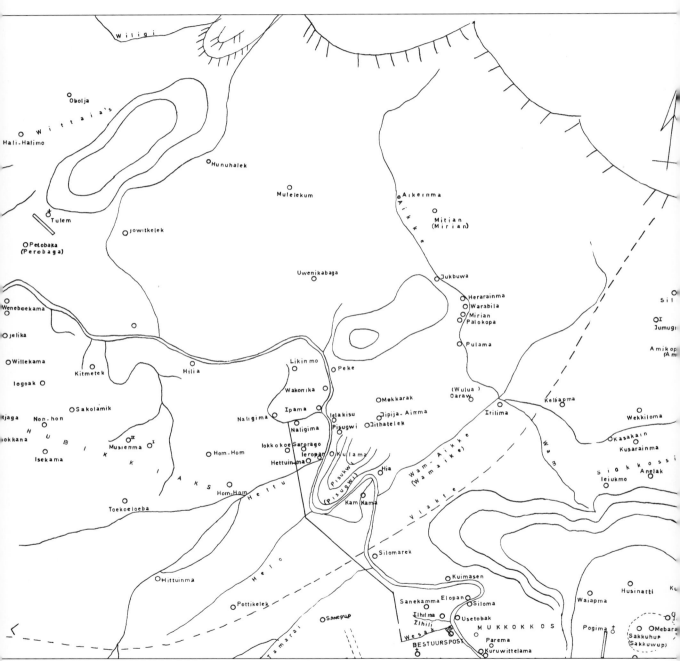

Official Netherlands New Guinea map of the northeastern Baliem Valley in 1960

no. 3, pp. 320–24. I have also enclosed a set of excerpts from missionaries' reports and letters over the past few years.

The *Handbook* is a Netherlands government handout and simply summarizes some of the basic data on weather, demography, and so forth. The other pamphlet is a pretty thin but probably accurate introduction to the zoology of Netherlands New Guinea. On this point I want to relate a remark made in conversation by Dr. Thomas Gilliard, the ornithologist at the [American] Museum of Natural History. He said in reply to my stating that our intention included a sort of ecological study of a small community, that the basis for an environmental approach had been magnificently laid by a series of large-scale zoological expeditions to contiguous areas led by a man named Archbold. I would like to suggest that you look up the publications that have come out of the Archbold Expeditions. As far as the language of these people is concerned, it is my hope that all of us will learn as much as possible before leaving.

July 8, 1960

de Bruyn to RG

Thanks for your letters bringing the good news that your plans are developing satisfactorily. I do hope that everything will run according to schedule and that we can welcome you here in March or April next year.

I recently had a talk with Mr. Broekhuyse. I advised him also to write to you as there are a few things he would like to know. He is a capable and at the same time enthusiastic person who will undoubtedly be of great assistance.

By this time, Michael was learning to do sound recording. He supposed that, inasmuch as he would be at the 1960 Republican National Convention, which bore significantly on his father's presidential ambitions, it would be a fine occasion to do some practice recording.

July 11, 1960

RG to Rockefeller

De Bruyn sounded extremely enthusiastic and promises to help all he can.

The Nagra is now purchased and delivered. As I look at it and think about it going to the Republican convention, I get very nervous. Even such a well-behaved political party as the Republicans must have its ruffians, and we would be really lost if this unit was stolen or damaged. I have another portable that you can take, if you will agree that its substitution is a good idea. Sam and I expect to drive down to New York City Monday night, July 18th, to see the Nikon and the camping goods people the next day. Will this date find you available?

July 15, 1960

de Bruyn to RG

When Monday night 10:30 p.m. the phone rang it was the first time in my 22 years in New Guinea that someone called me from the U.S.A. It was good to hear your and Dr. Brew's voices and to learn the good news that the plans for the film expedition to this territory are running according to schedule and that the necessary financial arrangements have been made.

A few days ago Mr. Broekhuyse, who came to Hollandia [the Dutch capital of Netherlands New Guinea, now known as Jayapura City], and I discussed the area where your expedition could best work. The best group to work among is the Kurelu group in the northern part of the Baliem Valley, east of Pyramid Mountain. There are no administration and mission stations in the area. The Kurelu group is the least culturally corrupted in comparison with other groups in the Baliem Valley, like those around Wamena and Pyramid, where we have had mission stations and later on administration stations since 1954 and 1956.

July 17, 1960

Jan Broekhuyse, in New Guinea, to RG

Last week I was in Hollandia and heard some details of your film expedition to the central highlands. I am going to join your party and will try to get as much information about the Dani population as possible.

At this point I was not only confident of the viability of the New Guinea trip, but also beginning to look more carefully at the kinds of claims and the validity of the reports coming to me from CAMA and other missionary organizations. Indeed, it was probably the beginning of what would turn into a long and sometimes contentious relationship with missionaries over the wholly different premises and intentions of our separate objectives.

July 19, 1960

RG memorandum of conversation with Mr. Christman, CAMA

Mr. Christman thought that we were going to the Baliem at an opportune moment as great change was being wrought in the lives of the natives—"Praise to the Lord."

In 1956, Christman was greeted at the Pyramid airstrip by 1500 natives all equipped for war—spears, arrows, and war paint. In 1960, Christman was met by an equally large crowd of natives, but this time they carried no war equipment. Although Christman could not claim that the natives had been made Christians, he felt that they were beginning to lose their warring ways. Unfortunately, for the CAMA, not all the people of the Baliem were as peaceful as those around the Pyramid station. Acculturation has proceeded at a fairly rapid rate around the missionary stations. There the missionaries have brought in seeds, western livestock, etc. Since 1958, there have been no indications of cannibal feasts.

Letter from Rev. Anderson
Dated - Jan.2, 1960

"The week after we wrote to you some natives who were not numbered among the baptized
Christians came from the Ilaga - valley to the west of the Baliem - to the north Baliem
about a days walk from the Ibele. They were telling the people there about the spiritual
awakening in the Ilaga and either they themselves had not come to understand the truth of
the gospel or else there was confusion in the minds of the hearers. The story came here
that the people would burn their charms and magical things; then they would get new
skins, presumably white, which everyone here seems to desire, and theold women would
become young again like when they were first married. The people here were quite excited
about it and were asking if it were the truth. We had tried to explain that God gives
us a new nature here and then when we die we go back to be with Him. We get not only
new skins but new bodies that willnever die or grow old again. Let us continue to pray
and be sobre and vigilant because Satan is not going to give up his hold on this area and
people easily. On Dec. 15 were awakened at 5:30 AM by battle screams. 2 of our local
men were on their way to their gardens to check the area to make sure the enemy were not
there so that the women and children could go to work. When they were ambushed, one
was speared in the neck and through the lower part of his leg. During the night some
men from the enemy group had sneaked down and were hiding in the tall grass. In a few
minutes men were racing from every direction for the battlefront. They gathered as
quickly on the other side and fought on until 10:00 AM; until the people on this side
killed one or two of the enemy and then the enemy group retreated to their own area.
The people here are on constant watch gecause there are numerous rumors that the
enemy group are coming back for revenge.

Letter from a missionary to his headquarters, 1960

Health conditions—Christman noted that dysentery was particularly bad at the Rose missionary camp and that nothing could be done to stop it. The people at the station had to build up an immunity to it and take extra precautions with drinking water. There is an excellent Dutch doctor at the Pyramid station. In Hollandia there is one of the best hospitals in the Far East.

Languages of the Baliem were being mastered by the CAMA missionaries under the expert guidance of Bromley. Bromley has discovered that of the twelve languages in the valley three are basic, and if these three could be learned a man could travel anywhere in the Baliem Valley, even into the Yalimo Valley to the Northeast.

August 6, 1960 **de Bruyn to RG**

The language of the Kurelu group is the same as that around Wamena, in which surrounding we originally planned to work. Mr. Broekhuyse is now concentrating on the study of the Kurelu culture.

Mr. Broekhuyse just wrote that the best inducement goods are cowrie shells *(Cyprea moneta)* and the *Cymbium diadema* shells. The latter are big shells with a diameter of twelve to fifteen inches. From these shells the Dani people cut oblong pieces which they use for necklaces. These *mikak* as they are called are very much in demand. 50 to 100 of these shells will provide a wealth of goodwill.

To obtain an interpreter is the biggest problem, as there are no Dani people who have a working knowledge of Dutch, English, or Malay. Mr. Broekhuyse himself is studying the language and will help you with interpretation, but it would be very handy if the other expedition members would know some Dani.

August 9, 1960

RG to Broekhuyse

We are coming to New Guinea to make a cinematic and photographic study of one small village or society. We are not making a film about Dani culture or a travelogue about New Guinea. We want to settle down in a village and stay there for several months. The place we go to must not be affected by the government or the missionary activity in the area. We are going to learn about the Dani not to change their way of life. We are going as "anthropologists."

The information that is most desperately needed is on the language. We have got to have language material (on tape and on paper) which is applicable to the area we are going to.

I certainly hope that you can make the contact, on an anthropological basis, with these people. It seems to me that you can be of immense and really indispensable assistance by starting anthropological research at the place where we will join you later on. Obviously we are going to need extremely good rapport and this cannot be done overnight. However, if you were able to start now, such rapport should be possible within the succeeding five or so months until we arrive.

I am sending you some Kodachrome film to take pictures hopefully in the area we shall be visiting. When and if you get to the Kurelu again, take pictures which are inclusive of large areas of the village and show what is going on, i.e., how the houses are located in relation to each other, how people circulate, where the fields are in relation to the houses, etc.

I am delighted that the contact between us is now made. We must continue to exchange information.

August 25, 1960

Broekhuyse to RG

The Kurelu area is not affected by missions and was only a few times visited by patrol officers. People speak the Wamena dialect of the Dani language. I had a call on radio with Myron Bromley who told me that Mrs. Rose had already sent language material to you in the States.

My approach to Kurelu will not be one of a government official, i.e., a patrol officer, but anthropological from the beginning on. Maybe when I enter the area *the people do not want me* so that I cannot contact them. But as already said, with the anthropological approach I hope to succeed and there is a big chance that it will be possible.

RG to Broekhuyse

It is very nice to be able to make definite progress on the language. We have received the mid-valley recording and corresponding written sheets from Mrs. Rose.

Slowly a more distinct picture of the valley emerges from the variety of information I have received. The prospect of the Kurelu area as a place to work is most pleasing, as I think I may already have told you. At this point, I would like, if possible, to make a start on getting some basic information about the culture. If there are any reports or descriptions written by you, even if they are very general, I would like them. Some of the kinds of things I should like to know are settlement patterns (i.e., how many, on average, people to a village, how many houses, how big an area occupied by the dwellings, etc.). If you could include illustrative photographs of village size and layout, this would be very useful. I want also to know how stable the population is (i.e., do people move from place to place, exchanging visits, or go on war parties, etc.). Next, I should like to know who lives in what houses (e.g., men by themselves, children by themselves, etc.). Next, who are and what makes certain individuals more authoritative or powerful politically than others? Next, what is the agricultural calendar (i.e., when do they prepare fields, when do they plant, when do they harvest, etc.)? Next, what is the ritual calendar (i.e., are there definite months or weeks when certain ceremonies are held, e.g., agricultural rites, initiation, marriage, etc.)? Next, how much activity is there at night as opposed to day? What is their sleep-waking cycle? What musical instruments do they use and who (men, women, children, specially trained musicians) plays them? Do they have a creation myth and what is it? (This is quite important to me, if you can possibly find it out.) Why and how often do the Kurelu attack other groups? Is there any cannibalism among them? Are there any definite and established trade links between the Kurelu and others (please give details about what is traded and how far)?

These are all very general questions, but if you can answer them even sketchily, I will have something to start on as far as planning how to begin once we are there.

There are other more technical questions that I would also like answered. What, in your opinion, is going to be the reaction on the part of the Kurelu to being quite thoroughly photographed? How much do you think they will want to be treated medically? Is the water in the Kurelu area plentiful and of good drinking quality? How much of a problem might pilferage and petty thievery be?

I suspect this is quite a bit to ask anyone in one letter. Please answer my questions as you get the information rather than waiting until most of it is in hand. I am, of course, getting more and more enthusiastic as time goes on and I certainly look forward to our future association and collaboration.

October 20, 1960

Broekhuyse to RG

Six rolls of Ektachrome film entered into a swamp near Kurelu like all my things. With the remaining film I will continue work.

Until now I have not written reports about Dani culture. I hope to be ready with a first preliminary report in the month of November. Do not think that it is a work that can be fitted into a few weeks; it continues stone by stone. Nevertheless, as soon as possible you will receive information.

Pilferage will not be a great problem but we will have to look after our things. Some police boys (carefully selected) will stay with us without disturbing our work.

Cyprea moneta. The ones that are not *Cyprea moneta* are *useless.* The bigger the shell the more value. Important is that I forgot to tell you about the little *nassa* [small snail] shell. I never used them because I could not get them. It is a *very beloved* shell. The people make the *walimoken* (chest ornament) from this sort of shell.

October 24, 1960

RG to Broekhuyse

I am sorry to hear the film went into a swamp. It makes me alert to new possibilities as far as our own equipment is concerned. I shall take what precautions we can.

I think we will be able to have [ornithologist and Smithsonian director] Dillon Ripley's two Ambionese helpers. De Bruyn will contact you about it. Since we will have them to help, I want to avoid bringing any "police boys," unless you are *absolutely* certain they are so good that we will have no trouble with them as far as "rapport" is concerned.

I have spoken to the Curator of Mollusks at Harvard about the *nassa* shells you mention. This is a large genus (over 100 species), so I must receive from you one of the *nassa* shells they like. Please send it immediately because it will take time to find a supply in this country. Please tell me, too, what amount I should bring.

I hope you will soon be able to answer some of the questions on Kurelu ethnography which I asked you in a letter sent September 2, 1960.

The issue of barter goods such as shells was one that I was able to solve quite easily once I had found, in Newton Upper Falls, Massachusetts, of all places, a collector of the most prized of all the shells we wanted to take, the Cymbium diadema. I think I was able to buy for very little about two or three dozen immense specimens. There is no question that these shells opened a way into the hearts of the most important and ordinarily most hostile Dani kains ("big men").

In the back of my mind there was always the thought that were I for any reason to decide against or be prevented from going to the Baliem, there was the alternative of working with the Asmat people of New Guinea's south coast. This is where Pierre-Domenique Gaisseau had made a vivid if also sensationalistic film called Le Ciel et la Boue *(known as* The Sky Above, the Mud Below *in its American release.) Gerbrands I knew to be entirely willing, even hopeful, of my coming where he was working, realizing the possible synergies that could mean. Gaisseau's film had impressed me, and the thought of working with preliterate artists in a headhunting society was quite intoxicating. And so it was that I kept in close touch with Gerbrands as my fate was being decided.*

October 26, 1960 | **Gerbrands, in New Guinea, to RG**

In a few days we are leaving by boat from Merauke for the Asmat, which will take two or three days depending on the weather.

It might be useful to tell you just one or two of my impressions of this country in view of yourself going on much the same track as I am going. An important thing is, that our experience has shown it to be rather a must for any expedition of some scale to have an able organizer on the spot well in advance. On the spot in your case meaning Hollandia. For it has turned out extremely difficult, if not impossible, to obtain exact and matter-of-fact information on nearly everything of importance for such an undertaking. Information is very often flatly contradictory, and mostly rather hazy. The only way to cope with this kind of problem is to scrape together many small bits of information and to put these together like a jigsaw puzzle. In your case I would advise you *strongly* to make yourself a short reconnaissance trip to the Baliem as soon as you arrive in Hollandia.

October 28, 1960 | **de Bruyn to RG**

I had a long talk with Broekhuyse, who just came down to Hollandia from a patrol to the Kurelu area. His recent patrol to this area where your expedition plans to work makes a change as to the location for operation necessary. Broekhuyse and his two policemen were received very unfavorably, if not hostilely, in the Kurelu area. There was at the moment a war raging between two large groups involving some 2400 men, he said. The natives were very uncooperative and even had serious objections to making pictures.

This letter both encouraged and depressed me. I was encouraged to know the Kurelu were practicing ritual war, and depressed to think we might not be able to take up residence in that part of the valley. I hoped that the designation "Kurelu" was one that was wide enough to leave some part of it accessible to me for filmmaking. I was in the grip of almost obsessive thinking, in which naïveté combined with ambitious goals had me supposing that a film concerned with hand-to-hand violence with ritual purpose could speak in a general way to the understanding of human aggression.

31

November 7, 1960 **RG to de Bruyn**

I received your rather distressing news about the Kurelu area the other morning and have spent considerable time since then attempting to grasp its full significance.

Let me say first that I have always considered it your prerogative to choose the place to which we should or could go. At the same time I have felt that you well understood the sort of conditions, culturally speaking, that we wanted to encounter. I am on record in my letters to you as rather adamant on the point that our enterprise be from start to finish anthropologically motivated and executed. I want no missionaries or police on the party nor do I want to be near an establishment which they maintain. I would like to ask that no definite spot be chosen now but that we have several possibilities in mind for the time when I come out and can go to some of these places and talk about them with you and Broekhuyse.

I think that you know it was my hope to settle in one place and stay there. I do not want to do any sort of "coverage" of the whole Valley. However, if in the place we chose to stay the men or women who live there are used to visiting or trading in another area, then, of course, I would like to move *with them*.

As you also know, it has been my hope that we might work on the theme of inter-group hostility. Since this is now an issue of such crucial world significance, it is timely that we explore a microcosm of it. With this in mind, I am anxious to go to that part of the Valley where the people are not under the direct influence and supervision of the government.

November 11, 1960 **Broekhuyse to RG**

I just moved to Wamena. I have all my time available for the expedition. I have included the *nassa* shell specimen. 20 kg will be sufficient.

November 15, 1960 **RG to de Bruyn**

I am sending you in this letter (1) list of crates being sent to your attention which contain our equipment and supplies; (2) list of the contents of these crates. Crates #s 1, 2, 3, 4, 5, 6, and 7 *MUST BE REFRIGERATED*. Crates #8–#23 do *not* require refrigeration but should be stored in a more or less dry environment, if possible.

I would greatly appreciate it if this shipment was left unopened until my arrival. I am always fearful that something will get broken or that film will be exposed by error. The only other dangers are high voltage or magnetic fields coming in contact or being in close proximity to the delicate recorders and cameras, or x-rays exposing the film.

NOV 18 1960

UNITED STATES ARMY

End of Basic
Eve of Devens

Dear Bob:

To my extreme relief my orders have finally come through for Fort Devens. As Sam might have told you I had been recommended for training as a Teletype repair-man. Whether my New York unit arrived at this on the basis of my skill as a sound recordist (which I convincingly described on all possible forms) or some latent aptitude, I do not know. But my first reaction was one of terror. Teletype repair-man is a non-A.S.A. M.O.S. I pictured myself shipped off to Fort Leonard Wood, Okla-homa, or Fort Jackson, Kentucky, and immediately wrote a passionate letter to my A.S.A. Captain describing my utter incompetence in the recommended field. For whatever reason I am now about to be trained as a (code) Traffic Analyst, described in my orders as "SECRET and CRYPTOLOGICAL". Perhaps I will acquire useful radio training. At least my typing will get a good polishing.

Letter from Michael Rockefeller to Gardner, 1960

33

November 15, 1960

Rockefeller, at Fort Dix, New Jersey, to RG

Since my orders for [Fort] Devens [in Massachusetts] do not go into effect until the 19th, I am now a holdover (otherwise known as "left-over" or simply "hang-over") for one week. This will be a week of occasional details, harassing the new cycle of recruits (joy), and, I hope, opportunity to get re-involved with anthropology.

You were quite right in your anticipation that I would have little free time while in basic training. Yet beyond my first three days at the Reception Center where Hurricane Anna acted as master of ceremonies, the army has actually been, from many points of view, a valuable experience. It has taught me some of the assets of a highly ordered day-to-day existence. I have received all sorts of useful pointers for field life in New Guinea from such things as bivouac and courses in first aid, land navigation, etc. Furthermore, I am in sterling condition.

I certainly appreciate the ceaseless work that I know you have done over the past two months. I only wish I could have been less of a dead weight. A class "A" pass giving me afternoons and evenings off after classes, and weekends after 4:30 Fridays, I hope will enable me to hold up my end of the rope while at Devens. I ought to get this pass next Wednesday, at which point I shall head immediately for Cambridge and the Peabody.

November 16, 1960

RG to Gerbrands

Many thanks for your very thoughtful letter. As for the "organizer" on the spot before setting forth, I fear that will have to be me. No doubt you know that de Bruyn has to go to New York in March for U.N. meetings. All of our equipment has finally been boxed and now awaits a ship.

November 23, 1960

de Bruyn to RG

Location for operation. The decision as to the area where your expedition will operate is *not* my prerogative but yours. The only thing I do is advise you where to go and not to go. Broekhuyse is working now in Minimo [in the mid-valley area]. The culture of the Baliem Valley including the Kurelu area is quite a homogeneous one. It may be possible that in April when the expedition starts the situation in the Kurelu region is such that the people are willing to cooperate. Broekhuyse's study in the Minimo area could also be used in case you are able to work in the Kurelu region.

You wrote that you plan to work on the theme of inter-group hostility. The cultural focus of the Baliem people is, as you know, traditional warfare. An anthropological film will automatically deal with this traditional animosity between the various groups.

For this territory you need a visa. The quickest way for you is to arrange this with the Netherlands Consulate General in New York.

34

November 28, 1960   **RG to Gerbrands**

I once told you that one of the members of our party was the son of Nelson Rockefeller, the governor of New York. His name is Michael Rockefeller, and he has many of his father's interests and talents with regard to art.

Michael and I were talking about New Guinea the other day, and as I described you and your research he became more and more interested in meeting you and visiting the Asmat area. Do you think that it would be possible for him to come down—say between mid-April and mid-May for a little while? I can assure you that he knows how to take care of himself and would be not the slightest burden. I think, if he had this opportunity, that it could possibly mean something in terms of the progress of research in the field of primitive art.

Gerbrands agreed to be Michael's host and guide when he and his friend Sam Putnam took two weeks in the midst of their highland work to go to the Asmat. I know that Gerbrands gave both of them as good advice as anyone could have and rekindled Michael's deep interest in the indigenous art he would see. Unhappily, Gerbrands had returned to Holland before Michael set forth the second time, after the Baliem Valley work had ended. The story of that second and fatal journey is yet to be reliably written.

December 3, 1960   **RG to de Bruyn**

I received your letter this morning answering my several questions. (This is the fastest trip any of our letters has made—a mere ten days!) Many thanks for your clear and concise treatment of all my queries.

Since I now know that you will be in Hollandia through the first week of April, I can start to plan my own arrival well enough in advance of your departure to consult at some length. Let's leave the precise area in which we are to stay undecided as you suggest. I would hope to make at least one reconnaissance to the Baliem with Broekhuyse and/or you to get a better idea of the possibilities.

Unfortunately we are unable to send an ethnologist early. By the way, I believe you do not know who it is to be. His name is Karl Heider and he is a Peabody-trained archaeologist-ethnologist. His interests lie in material culture and general ethnography. The plan is to have him come about the middle of March, enter the field about April 1st, and remain—with a few breaks for recreation and consolidation of work—for one year and a half. This will be necessary in order to do the thorough sort of material culture study that he intends. Also, he will be a continuous link to these people should we decide, of course with your concurrence, to return in the summer of 1962 for more photographic work.

December 18, 1960   **Gerbrands to RG**

I just received your letter of November 28th regarding the coming of Michael Rockefeller to the Asmat. Of course he is welcome! But why aren't you coming, both of you?

A fortnight ago I started field-work in the village of Ammanamgai on the Kampong River near to where it joins the South Eillanden River. I have a house, native style, where I can easily house two additional people, if they bring along their own cots and mosquito netting. Food is not necessary, provided my guests like sago, rice, shrimp, bananas, fish, pork, casuary [cassowary] meat, papaya, and perhaps sago worms. If I knew for certain when you would arrive in Agats, I would gladly come there and bring you to Ammanamgai by canoe. It is two days rowing, with a night stop halfway. If you would like a really profound impression of the Asmat, you should come by canoe and stay a couple of weeks with me. The people so far are the most friendly, hospitable, and intelligent I have ever met. It is really one of the most exciting experiences of my life to work with them.

December 22, 1960   **RG to Rockefeller**

Here is a tape. If you can learn all this you're red hot. I'm also enclosing some vitamin pills donated by Upjohn Co. Use them if you want to. There is a pill for every day in New Guinea.

January 3, 1961   **Broekhuyse to RG**

This morning I got a list of questions. Most of them can have a short answer—in a few weeks my report will be ready and give you more details.

Music instruments: There is only a little mouth harp about 10–15 cm long. People play individually.

Dances: The big dance is the victory dance *[etai]* after war. Several hundreds of men and women dance on a fixed place in open air. The dance is very simple, i.e., going around right to left or vice versa.

People sing on a lot of occasions, in practically all the ceremonies mentioned above and very much just for fun because they like it. There is always one who sings and one who answers.

Primitive art: The Dani are stone-age people and have very little of what we would call art. Most things are made by hand without decoration. The only decoration I have seen up to now is a little on the arrows and a rather abstract figuration on the water bottles. The biggest and nearly only decoration the men use is the *innumossi*—a sort of hat from pandanus leaves and fur. That's all.

January 18, 1961

RG to Brew

We have known for some time that the contact or rapport situation between the Dutch officials in the valley and the Dani has been pretty tenuous. In spite of this we had high hopes for some good material after a lengthy stay in one spot. For several months, however, as I read whatever I could about the Dani and their neighbors, and saw what few photographs had been taken, I grew increasingly concerned over what I tended to look upon as an "un-photogenic" situation.

What I want to point out is that the nature of film being what it is, a device primarily intended to capture action, it must necessarily be addressed to shapes and movement. If there is a paucity of variety to a culture's activities and appearance, there is bound to be a limit to the usefulness of photography. I get the impression from Broekhuyse that the major categories of physical activity are rather un-dramatic. It must also be considered that one of our main ambitions was to document the aggressive behavior of these people. However, it seems to me more and more improbable that the Dutch will tolerate any raids or wars, much less our documenting them.

In view of what, admittedly inferentially arrived at, seem to be the conditions we will encounter, I want to prepare you for a shift of focus, from the Baliem to the Asmat. I feel confident that de Bruyn will cooperate. I have laid the groundwork over a long period of time with Gerbrands (now in the Asmat) to meet just such a contingency as I see could arise.

January 23, 1961

B. J. Slingenberg, Consul General of the Netherlands, to RG

With reference to your application for a visa for Netherlands New Guinea and those of Messrs. Michael C. Rockefeller, Karl G. Heider, Samuel M. Putnam and Eliot Elisofon, I have the honor to inform you that on presentation of the passports the visa will be issued for a stay of six months.

January 25, 1961

Brew cable to de Bruyn

Gardner arriving Hollandia February 15. He is anxious to visit Baliem and Asmat in your company between February 15 and March 15, if at all possible. SS *Schielloyd* estimated to arrive with expedition crates first week in February.

January 25, 1961

RG to Rockefeller, in New York

Jo and I have sent a cable to de Bruyn saying that I will arrive in Hollandia the 16th of February wanting to go to the Baliem and the Asmat. We decided to say nothing about our worries over the Baliem situation until we got face to face. Keep going on [learning] Dani because the chances still are that we will go there.

37

Gardner during a lull in a ritual battle

in new guinea

February 15, 1961
RG's journal

Hollandia is a curious place. On a public monument I read: "Hollandia 1910–1960." The sign, which almost says everything, is a kind of gravestone, since no one sees any future for this island, certainly none for the Dutch as masters.

Getting from Cambridge, Massachusetts, to Hollandia, New Guinea, almost fifty years ago was simpler than it is now. KLM flew to Hawaii from New York and then from Hawaii to Biak, a desolate little island turned into an air base by the United States during World War II. From Biak, Kroonduif (Dove Air), a subsidiary of KLM, flew to Sentani, General Douglas MacArthur's headquarters in New Guinea for much of the war with the Japanese. From Sentani it was a half-hour car ride to the coastal city of Hollandia.

February 17, 1961
RG, in Hollandia, to Karl Heider, in Cambridge

I have been here two days, and this is really the first opportunity I have had to send you any word. The choice as to where we will work rests with us. De Bruyn completely understands the dilemma. There are many advantages to the Baliem. The transportation problem is much less acute—four flights a week to Wamena and government stores. In the Asmat one must wait a month for supplies, which can only reach the area by ocean-going vessels. The only other way is by charter floatplane at $100 per flying hour, and a round trip to Hollandia is about ten hours.

There is a radio and doctor at Agats and we would probably be no further than a day's canoe ride away. The material culture of the Asmat is very rich, including a stone axe culture, but it is more affected by other cultures (at least in the coastal areas) than the Baliem. The climate of the Asmat is very unhealthy, and the terrain is extremely difficult to negotiate on foot. Everything is swamp and mud. The native people in the Asmat are cooperative, in the Baliem they may not be.

I am leaving for the Asmat on the 23rd probably—connections are very uncertain. I shall stay two or three weeks. If it seems feasible to go there, we (you, Mike, and I) would take the boat around the island, Hollandia to Merauke, on the 6th of April. This takes about three weeks, which is unfortunate because it delays us so. If we go to the Baliem, there is no problem about delays; you could come in immediately. I shall not be able to give you an answer as to which place it will be until just before you leave. I will try to cable you by the 20th of March.

February 17, 1961
RG to Heider, second letter of the day

Since I wrote, it has been decided that de Bruyn and I will make a fast trip to the Baliem. We will probably go on Tuesday the 21st, talk with Broekhuyse and do some inspection, and then return on the following Friday, the 24th, in time to let me go to Merauke and the Asmat on Sunday the 26th.

February 23, 1961

RG, in Wamena, to Rockefeller, in Cambridge

My first impressions are very favorable. The Valley is an incredibly beautiful place, the natives are *not* drab, and the rhythm of their lives is far more energetic than I had supposed. They seem to have a quality of spontaneity and drive in everything they do; they fight hard, grieve deeply, laugh loudly, and, generally speaking, move quickly. The problems here would be rapport in an area unused to other cultures, the darkness and smallness of their houses, and the low concentration of people in a given settlement. I will know much more soon about this area and about the Asmat. All I am sure of now is that plans will change because that is the New Guinea pattern. I also know that you would be amazed and delighted by this Valley.

February 24, 1961

RG to Heider

I have been here since Tuesday. Wamena is nothing more than an unsightly cluster of aluminum buildings looking more like motels than anything else, and a transient population of Dani wanting to work for a few Dutch cents a day. The valley and river are both magnificent. I have seen little more than the mid-valley section so far and very little beyond the shores of the Baliem. It is the only properly navigable waterway, so that wanting to work on a tributary usually means walking along its banks, not sailing on it.

Government rest house in Wamena, 1961

The sun is much stronger—when it shines—than I had reckoned. I now look at the world through lobster-red and swollen eyelids. I would advise you to bring a tube of sunburn cream. Also, be sure to bring a cap or hat.

I have decided nothing about where we should work. I would like to wait for the south coast, which, by present plans, I will visit starting March 9th. I will be here February 28th to March 6th in order to go with Broekhuyse to the Kurelu. Incidentally, I think if we are to work here, Broekhuyse will be enormously helpful and enjoyable.

There is practically nothing known about this area. Kurelu is both a "big man" and an area. He is reputedly fierce and warlike as well as opposed to the administration. People are being killed quite regularly in his territory and along his borders. I saw his area through binoculars when we climbed some hills in back of Tulem [a missionary station in the territory of the Wittaia, enemies to the Willihiman-Wallalua in Kurelu]. The whole valley is very flat and broad until you get out to the foothills of the high escarpments that surround it. I believe we shall try to make contact with one of the villages part way up the side of the hills in back of Kurelu. It would be well to be enough above the valley floor to be out of the mud and able to

Kurelu at a ritual battle

survey the fronts along which the war activity will take place. A good deal depends on Kurelu's willingness to cooperate, and to try to induce this we will bring some of the bigger diadema shells they admire so much. I gather from talking with missionaries and government people here that the valley is far from pacified. The somewhat bedraggled Dani living near the post [Wamena] must be viewed against the magnificent specimens that are manacled together in the jail compound a little way off.

I have seen Minimo, the village Broekhuyse has worked in, and got a good idea of the physical layout we would find anywhere. The houses are terribly small and dark. This would be a problem. There are an immense number of flies. There has been rain, 37mm since I arrived (there is as much or more in the Asmat). We will need police, but they will be dressed in mufti and trusted to mind their own business. Broekhuyse is very keen to go about things anthropologically and has a very strong sense of "academic" purpose. You must tell Mike, in answer to any question by anyone that our mission is to *study a culture*.

February 26, 1961   **RG, in Hollandia, to Heider**

The three days I spent in the Baliem were enormously instructive. They were also very wet, so wet that the DC-3 could not come in on the regular flight Friday. Fortunately, the missionary Cessna could, and we flew back in a way that gave a far better look at the terrain. I asked the pilot to take me over Kurelu's areas, and he obliged. There were some remarkable sights. There are about 200 watchtowers from which mutually hostile groups are kept under surveillance, lovely villages tucked into the notches between foothills, and fantastic villages crowning ridges like medieval fortress towns.

March 6, 1961   **RG, in Wamena, to Heider**

I flew up in the missionary Cessna. Broekhuyse and I set out for Tulem, where we expected to get carriers for the journey afoot to Kurelu. We arrived to discover no carriers were willing to venture across the Kurelu frontier. We made camp in a beautiful place atop the beginning of a long spur that stretches out toward Kurelu to the east. The next morning we had better luck and found enough people to take us all the way. At about one o'clock, after crossing an immense bog and swamp, the same that claimed Broekhuyse's film last summer, we reached the border of Kurelu. There were several villages to be seen from where we entered and the decision had to be made as to which we should go. Another half an hour and we were on top of another knoll, which this time looked west across the valley floor to the river and escarpment behind. Many men and boys had followed us and all were genuinely agog. There is no question that

Admiring a great shell *(Cymbium diadema)*

most had never seen white skin, tents, rope, etc. You must remember that the rule in the remoter parts of the valley is that people stay within their territorial limits.

The next day we continued our contact activities, bringing out one of the diadema shells. This, I'm convinced, did the trick. There was little question left concerning our welcome. With one man we concentrated on communicating our intention. He is very intelligent, sly, and opportunistic. He saw the chance that our being there with riches in shells was a way for him to gain in a short time the prestige, women, and renown he might otherwise wait a lifetime to get. It was this man, Wali, and another greater but more distant *kain* [strongman or leader], who offered to eat a pig with us. The eating of a pig is a sort of combination peace pipe smoking cocktail party reception. All I will say is that we ate both pigs, thus settling our affairs in Kurelu and, alas, unsettling our digestions. Both of us were violently and dismally sick. The place we are is definitely stone-age and uncorrupted. We have a very fine start in the valley, and I am most tempted. I leave for the Asmat Thursday.

March 8, 1961

RG, in Hollandia, to Timothy Asch, Film Study Center

Here are the first attempts at still photography. All were done between the 2nd and 6th of March. I think a couple of rolls never got exposed, because I had trouble with the advance lever. I have greater respect than ever for the still boys. It was not easy for me to learn what to do with my first 35mm camera. Let me know how things go with these rolls. I'm leaving for the Asmat tomorrow—back on the 24th of March. If something terrible is wrong, send a cable, but follow it up with a letter of explanation.

The only way of reaching the Asmat, on the southern coast, from Hollandia was by taking a flight to Merauke, a district center from which boats radiated out along the coast to the east and the west. De Bruyn asked a linguist interested in Papuan languages to accompany me, supposing that his Dutch, English, and Malay would be more useful than my English, French, and a little German. On arrival in Merauke we spent a night before boarding the government boat scheduled to leave the following day.

March 10–19, 1961

RG's journal, written aboard the government boat bound for Agats in Asmat territory

Asmat society, like many other New Guinea societies, puts an enormous premium on masculinity, causing women all over this island to have a dreadful and secluded time of it. Wherever men go, be they Asmat or Dutch, women react shyly and recede quickly into the background. There seems here to be little communication between the sexes and I foresee difficulties for anyone wanting to show some form of affection. The men in their ample spare time are usually in the *jeu* [men's house]. They take their male children there and sleep, carve, eat, talk, and do ceremonies. They seem not to be interested in work except when it is absolutely necessary. There was a time when their efforts were periodically devoted to hunting heads. Such undertakings are, with the exception of a raid a few months ago well up the river from Ammanamgai, the exception these days. Men still keep the skull of an enemy they once killed, but it is supposed there is far less of this activity nowadays.

My visit to Adrian Gerbrands and the chance to see under expert guidance the astonishingly rich art making of the Asmat people was both a great pleasure and necessary to making the decision about my working destination.

Unquestionably, the interest I had in the Asmat came not only from their splendid expressiveness in sculpture, painting, and song, but also from a deep vein of violence running through their religious belief system. Headhunting was a way of life that found its meaning in an elaborate cosmology. I wondered, too, whether it might not be more evidence of a universal human taste for blood. It was interesting to have to decide between two cultures in which violent behavior was sanctioned by largely religious principles. It is also interesting to live in a time at the start of the 21st century when great powers (Arab, Israeli, and American) share such proclivities. My pursuit of these tendencies in human behavior could probably have been satisfied in both the Asmat and the Baliem, and I frequently regretted not having had the opportunity or the strength of purpose to make two films.

March 18, 1961

RG, in Agats, to Brew, Peabody Museum

Considering the immense difficulty confronting the orderly, or even just partly organized, man in New Guinea, my time and efforts have been used to an incredibly efficient degree. As you perhaps realize from piecing together my scattered communications, I have managed two separate and different sorts of visits to the Grand Valley, one with Vic de Bruyn and a longer one with Broekhuyse. I will manage the same sort of thing here, having just returned from a tremendously enjoyable short week of inspection of the southeast Asmat with Gerbrands. I will leave, probably this evening, on another tour, again with Gerbrands but also in company of a government linguist. I have just sent the cable to de Bruyn for transmittal to you that we will work in the Grand Valley. I would never have made the decision without coming here and would always have been nagged by doubt in my choice, if I had not come. Not everything weighs in favor of the Baliem, but more than enough. Broekhuyse looks *very good*. He and I made a highly successful contact in the Kurelu, which is very much unaffected by other cultures. Conditions for a party our size are much more favorable in the valley, and perhaps more important, we have access to the Dani culture both linguistically and

Abandoned *bisj* poles in the Asmat village of Otsjanep

45

ethnographically, which, despite the more advanced state of acculturation in the Asmat, is not possible there.

March 22, 1961

Brew to RG

We have received a cable from de Bruyn saying that you have decided on the Baliem. Your letters to Karl paint a really attractive picture of Kurelu. I am sure that, anthropologically speaking, this is infinitely superior. If that is the case, and with your skills and the energies of your staff, you should come out with a most interesting and valuable film.

March 24, 1961

**RG, in Hollandia, to Asch and Carol Thompson
(RG's assistant at the Film Study Center)**

I just sat down to a feast of letters that have been waiting until I got back, this morning, from the Asmat. I'm keeping a journal and having a hard time doing it and everything else. I'm afraid I'll have to give you the scene in bits and snatches.

The Asmat was hot, hip deep in mud, and crawling with crocodiles and headhunters. The crocodiles come out at night, and so I only saw pairs of greedy red eyes. The headhunters only come out by day, when they know there might be a white man coming along with some tobacco, for which they eagerly sell their trophy heads.

I meet Karl and Mike at the airport day after tomorrow. It will be nice to luxuriate in the English language again.

A footnote to the Asmat part of this story is that Professor William W. Howells, a physical anthropologist at Harvard, had asked Michael Rockefeller to procure a collection of Asmat skulls presumably taken by headhunters. I am not sure what the outcome of this negotiation was, but I do know that Asmat men who owned one or more heads taken in hand-to-hand combat, as was the correct ritual practice, were quite willing in 1961 to sell them for a few yards of nylon fishline or chunks of tobacco.

March 25, 1961

RG to Asch

I am sending a small package of 35mm rolls to you today. These I pretty much shot on the run in the Asmat. I was limited to the 35mm lens because the zoom lens is just too impractical.

The time draws closer to when we will be in the field. I tested the cameras today and am waiting until a nice Papuan technician finishes developing them.

I hope everything is going well for you and John on the Bushman material. I hate, in one way, the thought of more material coming into the Center before the footage we have is finished with—but I also see that this is pretty much a last chance in New Guinea, at least.

Victor de Bruyn, Gardner, and
Rockefeller at Sentani

Departing Sentani for Wamena

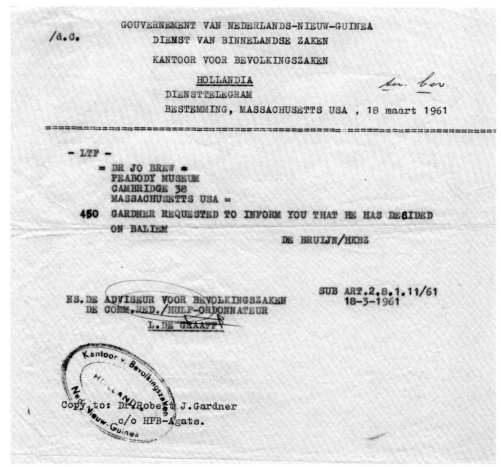

Cable from Gardner to Brew

RG, in Wamena, to Brew

It is a vast, blue-skied, sun-smitten valley we have all finally reached and now take a little time to enjoy with rest and last minute preparations before setting out for the Willihiman-Wallalua [Dani clans living in the Kurelu area] the day after tomorrow at six a.m.

Mike and Karl have been duly initiated with a pig killing ceremony in our honor yesterday at a small village downstream. I took them there to get their feet and hands used to the shapes of houses and gardens before we go on to the Kurelu. I was very surprised to see what a large shell [that] we took to pay an important man for his work with Broekhuyse this past fall would do. In an instant a pig was in the air and in another an arrow was in its heart. The boys had a pretty full day watching all this and eating their first ceremonial sacrifice.

I should tell you a little more precisely where we will be and how we shall keep in touch. We will be seven hours' walk from Wamena, or seven hours by boat and a walk along the Aikhé River. I plan to send for messages, mail, and supplies every Saturday or every other Saturday, depending on urgency. We will monitor the government radio channels every morning and get cables and other messages. I have arranged to be left *completely* alone by the government and visitors such as newspaper and television people who come regularly to Wamena owing to tensions between Holland and Indonesia. Incidentally, the *New York Times* correspondent Homer Bigart did a big story on us, and you might watch for it these next two weeks or more. We seem to be spending well within our budget, so there is no cause for anxiety on that score.

I feel that Karl is going to have a great opportunity, with any luck and continued cooperation of the Willihiman-Wallalua, and I am convinced that Mike sees himself a fully participating and contributing member of the crew. It is hard to say when our first results will be coming in. This is like the first Bushman project, where reactions to cameras couldn't be calculated with any certainty.

RG's journal

Almost simultaneous with our arrival [on April 3rd] in the forest, an enormous roar came from a great distance. The thought that this might be a prelude to war went through everyone's mind, I am sure. The sound was full of exultation, preempting all other sounds normal to a noonday in the valley. Climbing to a place on the hill behind our camp, I could see out on the valley floor an immense cluster of dark motion—waves of bodies running in the shadows of a setting sun. We discovered it to be the start of a victory celebration. Recently, possibly on Easter, a Wittaia warrior had been killed by one of the Willihiman-Wallalua, the clan name of the Dani group on our side of the frontier.

Victory dancing

Harvard Expedition Discovers A Warrior Tribe in New Guinea

By HOMER BIGART
Special to The New York Times.

HOLLANDIA, Netherlands, New Guinea, March 27—A Harvard anthropological expedition, led by Robert G. Gardner, has discovered in the heart of Dutch New Guinea a savage tribe whose culture is focused on war —the Willigiman-Wallalua people in the lofty Baliem Valley. The tribe's warriors are judged by the number of enemy slain, the number of pigs stolen and the number of wives captured. Apparently they have no qualms about killing enemy women and children; these seem to add as much to their prestige as a slain male adult, according to Mr. Gardner.

Even their music is unconsciously aggressive. A good deal of it consists of grinding their teeth in harmony.

Michael Rockefeller, youngest son of Gov. Nelson Rockefeller and a member of the expedition, will make sound recordings of the teeth chatter and also of war chants, a medley of hoots and rumbles accompanied by an instrument resembling a jew's-harp.

Mr. Gardner and Jan Broekhuyze, a Dutch anthropologist, found the Willigiman-Wallalua on March 6. They were looking for a people called Kurelu in an uncharted part of the valley. Mr. Broekhuyze, in a previous attempt to reach the Kurelu, had been frustrated by inhospitable natives. But this time they were provided with sea-snail shells, on which the Baliem Valley tribes set great store.

"We were on the edge of a swamp when we first saw the natives," said Mr. Gardner, who is director of the Film Study Center at Harvard. "They were observing us from watchtowers twenty feet off the ground, which they had built by lashing some long thin trees together."

"They climbed down from the towers as we approached. Broekhuyze, who speaks the language of the Dani group quite well, began to talk to them. He opened with a traditional greeting and then ex-

New York Times article, April 5, 1961

April 4 and 5, 1961

RG's camera notes

Shot the first four rolls of film on an *etai* [victory dance]—everyone pretty subdued by us—only Polik (tall man, long hair, lovely headdress with vertical spire) seemed at ease and able to do some improvisatory dancing—the women are all quite unapproachable though not entirely lacking in healthy curiosity. The next day there was a larger and more vigorous celebration that continued to sunset—hard to get the feeling of arriving and departing cadres—want to get spears to tell the story by being planted when men arrive and picked out of the ground when they leave. Everything shot on the Filmo as it is my only camera so far—some problems with film take-up using old flanges—the last ten feet pile up—happened two or three times.

In a climate with as high humidity as that of the Baliem, it was inevitable that technical problems would occur. Motion picture film swells noticeably in damp conditions, and when it does the close tolerances of camera design frequently cause it to jam as it feeds through the transport mechanism. I was sure that this sort of problem would arise and managed to avoid some of the consequences, but I was not prepared for its relentlessness.

As for choice of camera, I was conservative in taking both battery (Arriflex) and spring-driven (Filmo) models. I was doubly conservative in taking two of each variety. Were I to have chosen a second time, I would have taken a Bolex instead of a Filmo. I had thought the Filmo more sturdy and less prone to failure, but the Bolex was and still is a better camera.

plained why we were there.

"The men became curious and put down their fifteen-foot spears. We crossed a swamp up to our knees in muck to some high ground where they were standing. There were about fifty warriors, some of them magnificent specimens 6 feet 3 inches tall.

A Warriod Led Them

"We found that they were not of the Kurelu, but an allied people. We explained that we wanted to live with them, and motioned to three or four hamlets we had observed up against a hill. We talked for half an hour. Finally, a young warrior who was acute enough to realize he had much to gain — we had shown him the sea-snail shells — led us to one of the hamlets."

Mr. Gardner and Mr. Broekhuyze pitched a tent, but there was little sleep for them the first night. The front of the tent was open and Mr. Gardner was acutely conscious of perhaps fifty pairs of eyes that followed his every move.

He heard a hissing intake of breath as he removed his shirt. "I think they were amazed that my whole body was white," he said.

Mr. Gardner recalled that when he first heard the teeth grinding he was unable to understand what the noise was. Then he noticed that the warriors were waggling their jaws in unison, like stenographers with chewing gum. "It wasn't very musical," he said, "but it helped them pass their time."

Mr. Gardner said that the men wore nothing but a loin covering made of gourds and the women were clad with the skimpiest of fiber skirts.

The men adorned themselves with pig grease and soot. Great gobbets of fatty soot hung from their hair and faces.

The sleeping arrangements were odd. All the men slept on a sleeping platform in a round house. Women, pigs and children slept in another common house. The men and women mingled in a third house, which the natives called Ebe-ai.

Women carried small pigs about, Mr. Gardner said, and generally wore three nets, one for the baby, one for the pig and one for sweet potatoes.

The expedition, which will last six months, is supported by the Peabody Museum of Archaeology and Ethnology at Harvard and by the Netherlands Government.

Other members of the team are Peter Matthiessen, naturalist and author, and Eliot Elisofon, photographer, who will join the party in mid-April.

April 4, 1961

Asch to RG

The color is fine on your returned transparencies. The exposure is excellent. We've seen some lovely photographs of the country and interesting photos of the people, especially at the pig feast you attended. The particularly nice shots were the details every time, for example, the closer shots of roof building and the close shots of people, especially in the evening light. The High Speed Ektachrome seemed to have a better color than the Kodachrome. Somehow it seems to me that the most valuable work that can be done with your 35mm equipment would be done very close to whatever activity you are photographing.

April 5, 1961

Rockefeller's sound-recording notes

These are the first sound tape recordings made in the Baliem Valley. The *etai* field was roughly as follows:

There were approximately 150 women and 400 men present. The men were dressed in their complete war attire (spears, bows and arrows, and all. The women and girls came in their normal skirts, but some had had their complete bodies painted in mud of red brown, yellow brown, or grayish colors. Tape 1—wind noise throughout. Tape 3—*some rich voices* without wind. Tape 5—at night, very low chanting, very high crickets—best singing at *etai* so far.

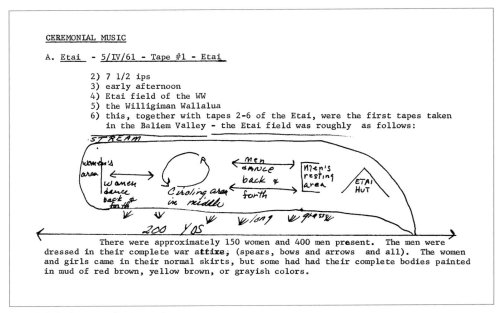

```
CEREMONIAL MUSIC

A. Etai  - 5/IV/61 - Tape #1 - Etai

        2) 7 1/2 ips
        3) early afternoon
        4) Etai field of the WW
        5) the Willigiman Wallalua
        6) this, together with tapes 2-6 of the Etai, were the first tapes taken
           in the Baliem Valley - the Etai field was roughly  as follows:
```

There were approximately 150 women and 400 men present. The men were dressed in their complete war attire, (spears, bows and arrows and all). The women and girls came in their normal skirts, but some had had their complete bodies painted in mud of red brown, yellow brown, or grayish colors.

Rockefeller's diagram of a victory dance

April 6, 1961

RG's camera notes

Continuation of the *etai*—this series has shots which get closer—am almost run over by herd of 100 warriors. Filmo somewhat bulky with zoom but it is very nice to get reflex and all focal lengths in one piece of glass. Still too early to pick out our closer friends—Wali, Jegé Asuk, etc. do not participate very actively. Tried some slow motion just to get a different slant on the chaos. Women far more approachable than two days ago, but details very hard to get as people of both sexes move when one gets too close, and the sound of the camera scares them off, if we don't.

April 7, 1961

RG to Brew

I shall try to put down a few thoughts at the end of four days in the field. These have been days full of hard work, nuisances, frustrations, and many different feelings, including elation. Broekhuyse, Michael, and I came by boat along the Aikhé River early Monday morning. We reached our campsite at about 2 p.m. There was time to raise only one tent, before both light and muscle gave out. Tuesday morning we started to make a more livable camp, and had scarcely begun when around noon the sounds of voices, carrying a very long distance, reminded everyone that the area we had come into was not yet pacified. Looking out over the broad valley floor from our position about 300 feet higher in the eastern foothills, we saw masses of men moving in reversing waves about four or five kilometers away. Noticing this, we asked what was happening and received the answer that because a Wittaia warrior had been slain the day previous to the day we arrived, there was as usual an *etai* or victory celebration. This *etai* has lasted for three days because another enemy has been slain, and I do not know yet whether or not it will continue tomorrow. We were able to make film, photographs, and sound recordings. The films and photographs will start for the Museum tomorrow. I can only say that 300–500 decorated and armed warriors dancing against 8000-foot peaks makes most spectacles I've seen pale by comparison. However, because of our recent arrival and that we are still strange to many of these people, especially the women, who are automatically shy and run at the sight of a camera, the photography was mainly from a distance.

In two caves about 1000 feet behind and above our camp as we walked home after a visit to another village, we saw charcoal drawings of human figures. And at both caves some of the teen-aged Willihiman-Wallalua boys who were helping us by carrying sacks and equipment, spontaneously began to draw these figures before our eyes. Hardly remarkable when it happens so casually, but I think it interesting to be in the midst of authentic neolithic art.

Our problems are not all solved by any means. We have barely adequate translation, our knowledge of cultural patterns is still quite sketchy, and information about when and where things are to happen is altogether haphazard and unreliable. I believe that except for such explosions as the *etai*, wars, or mayhem of one sort or another, the cameras will be relatively inactive for at least the next month.

I expect Eliot the first of May. It is a terrible pity he missed the fantastic glory of these last few days. Peter should come soon. We shall meanwhile soak up the daily life and as much language as possible.

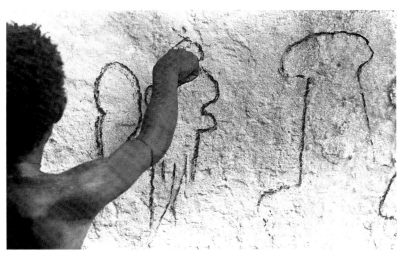

A child drawing with charcoal

The height of ritual battle

RG to Asch

The third shipment of exposed film material will be coming to you shortly after you get this note: there is both still and movie in this one. All the material is on the dance, which happened to begin almost the moment we arrived. It is called an *etai*, which means victory dance. It is celebrated when an enemy warrior is killed. The dance was spectacular—300 to 500 armed and feathered spearmen. Unfortunately we were not able to work close or coherently, because we were so new to these people and because I had no idea what was actually happening. There should be something, though. Please *cable* a few words when you see the work-print. Nearly all was handheld because I had no tripod until the last day, and everything was shot on the Bell and Howell [Filmo]. We are still moving in equipment, and it was only the greatest good fortune that I thought to bring any movie camera and film.

RG's camera notes

This is the first *weem* [battle]—astonishing affair—too bewildered to do much—hard to relate to the reality of it.

It is perhaps possible to see in the breathlessness of this note the power of the experience of seeing my first ritual war. I had been anticipating the moment for months, and doing so without any sense of what it would actually be like. All that I knew was contained in the two words: ritual and war. What I finally saw on April 10th was, in its clashing of arms and din of exultations, too overwhelming to comprehend.

RG to Asch

Things have been happening terribly fast. As you will see when this shipment is processed, we have had a very busy and exciting time. Please do not say anything about what is on the film. Consider all the material coming back highly confidential.

I'm terribly anxious to know about this stuff. I will assume it is OK—that is, I will go on with this subject. I could only handhold a Filmo—it will shake because I was shaking, and there will be light-struck parts when I had minor jams. I only pray some came out.

With this shipment of the first tentatively shot scenes of war on the 10th of April, shot despite my good intentions of lying low until some rapport had been built, the theme of the film I had come to make had begun to unfold. I was almost paranoid in thinking how I might be deprived of my good fortune, of how this first seemingly gratuitous few hours of outrageous luck might never return. This is the thinking of a filmmaker more than a disinterested observer—should there be such creatures—and I needed to swear my friends to silence lest I tempt the Fates.

April 12, 1961

RG's camera notes

Shot a sequence of Hanomoak, who was wounded by an arrow during the fighting on the 10th. The arrow went into his back and there is another wound in front on his right side where blood was let. The sequence was: walking to his *sili* [village unit], done three times, walking camera, going through entrance, going toward *honai* [men's house], at fence, picks pitch gum from *sien* [araucaria] tree, sits and plucks hair with it from his legs, goes into *honai*, comes out of *honai*, leaves *sili*. This roll was meant to provide some continuity on one of the warriors who took part in the battle—Hanomoak is a handsome, progressive-minded young man proud of his prowess as a warrior.

Tried to do a small operation on a man's foot to take out an arrow, but the wound had swollen too much and so abandoned the idea. For some days the young boys have been playing hard at their war games with straw spears and I have been trying to film this at different times of day—they tend to play late when the light is fine but often quite low—Warabara [hill and battlefield] in the background.

Do landmarks from the hill above camp, of Libarek [dance ground], the trail to salt wells, Warabara, gardens, main villages, etc. Do Jegé Asuk, Aloro, Wali, Weyak, Hanomoak, Uwar, Aplegma, etc. *just walking.*

Ask Jan and Abututi [our Dani interpreter]: (1) What do people really think of Wali? (2) What women are pregnant? (3) Is Uwar initiated? Who are his real father and mother? (4) Does Jegé Asuk have a wife? Where does he live? (5) Might a woman go to the salt wells while there is a battle? (6) Want a talk with Jegé Asuk. We were pretty clearly snake people [in Dani parlance the term used for Europeans], but now we seem to be pretty much accepted and so the control once exercised by Wali is slipping from his hands.

Wounded warrior returning from battle

April 13, 1961

RG to Brew

I am not able to give as much thought or time to these brief reports as I should like. As you can easily imagine, things are happening quickly and often unexpectedly. So far no one has had a moment to be bored, and few of us have had many moments to so much as reflect. Peter Matthiessen arrived exactly on schedule, the 10th, and has very quickly grasped the outlines and major threads of the life of these people so far as any of us can formulate them. Mike has shown himself to be a tireless walker and a willing worker. I suggested that he do some charting of our area from the high hills behind our camp and above most of the villages that surround us here on the valley floor. With his drawing skill and with the aid of photographs, we should have our location pretty well mapped in not too long a time. Karl has been busy in his caves, mentioned in my last letter, which now number at least three of artistic significance. Karl is also learning

Pua practicing to be a warrior

Jan Broekhuyse

language and helping with incidental photography. Broekhuyse is a great help and a fine companion for us all.

My own approach for at least the next three or four weeks is to absorb as much as possible. No certain film outline has yet emerged though several ideas are incubating, and of course several events of major proportions have transpired and have *had* to be filmed. You may be able to get a glimpse of these when the film I have sent back (around 3000′) has been processed and printed. I have told Tim to keep very quiet about what is on this film, because our final effort in a film or films to be eventually made could be blunted by an early disclosure of the material. Also, there may be some local political or governmental problems arising out of loose talk.

You may recall that I talked about making a film on the salt trade. I am happy to report, now that it is over, that I have made the journey, yesterday, to the major salt well in the northern part of the Grand Valley. It is a tiring three-hour walk from here, controlled by Kurelu, and visited by people as far away as the Yalimo, another valley two weeks walk to the east. The well is situated about 800–900 meters above the valley floor and presents one of the most interesting, almost supernatural, sights imaginable. Depending on luck and what reservoirs of energy we can call upon, there could certainly be a film on this topic.

Our relations continue to be almost terrifyingly good. I put it this way because our experience is so far so unlike that of anyone else in this area as to trouble me into supposing it could suddenly change. We hope not, and will take advantage of the situation as it now exists.

April 15, 1961

RG's camera notes

Second *weem*—even more astonishing. I have hopes that the material is superior to that shot on April 10th, both in pictorial quality and intelligibility. The first war was a sort of wild, incomprehensible sensation. The last one began to seem logical and reducible to certain principles or patterns. On the first roll there is material of Wali on his way to war, and waiting for it to begin. There is also material on people in *kaios* [watchtowers] and trees watching for developments. On one of the rolls there are shots of men going toward the battle-ground over fences and across ditches. Certain individuals besides Wali come in for concentration by the cameras—Aloro the crippled bowman, Jegé Asuk the prancing clown, Polik of the straight back, Uwar the enchanted but frightened boy. In one or two of the rolls there should be some good material of the skirmishing on the north side of the battlefield, where in the same shot both friend and foe can be seen enticing each other's fire. There is also some material of the wounded being carried back on the shoulders of comrades.

The battle proceeds and the wounded are carried home

The hard work of gardening

April 19, 1961	**RG's camera notes**

50 feet of Aloro, crippled warrior coming home from the frontier. 50 feet in early evening of the boys' spear game—tripod and wide-angle shots. More half-tripod and half-handheld to feature Uwar and one or two other boys (Uwar is a lefty and angelic looking). There is also material on Wali but he and I screw it up—he is just back from some real fighting—the Warabara should show in background.

April 19, 1961	**Rockefeller's sound-recording notes**

Boys playing war (*not* true sound synch). Approximately 20–25 boys, ages 8–14—taped in conjunction with movie camera. There were two sides. Their object was to simulate the kind of war in which their fathers indulged, as closely as possible. The charges, stalking, retreats, even the spears (made from the cane found in the field) were real in miniature. The sounds correspond to the progress of the battle, whether it be the swish of feet running through the field, the whoops of triumph occurring when an enemy is hit, or the shouts stimulated by a mass attack.

April 20, 1961	**RG's camera notes**

Shots on way to garden *kaios,* women working in fields (hard to start on this subject since the women are all so wary)—women coming home—Warabara in background—*kaios* and smoke—crossing log over ditch, shadows in water.

April 21, 1961	**RG's camera notes**

Boys on way to war. Uwar on hill behind Homoak (our camp) singing (this is recorded) joined by Aplegma.

These spare camera jottings reflect a time when the film was still finding its feet in terms of subject matter and structural devices on which the story would be built. I do not know whether I had by this time begun pondering the significance of the words "dead" and "birds." Somehow I don't think it was until the first funeral that they started to take on metaphorical significance.

April 21, 1961	**Rockefeller's sound-recording notes**

Uwar and Aplegma singing on a rock on the side of the slope to the south and behind the camp. Uwar was found alone singing. Bob called me to make a recording before he took some shots. By the time I was there with the recorder, Uwar's spontaneity was gone. He sang one phrase for me and then his friend Aplegma had to be called to accompany him. Most of the cut is of the two singing together. They insisted the song and sound had no name. The words were as follows:

Kere waliké keoe aho	We don't like to go far away
Kere heriké oe	We like to roam around
Kere heroké oe aho	nearby, not far away
Weke sop hano mike	It is good to close
Larogo kiriké aho	the door from the inside
Seten iwalogo	Let us build a brilliant
Kumusil logioe aho	fire so that we can see the women
Waliké, waliké	It is not good to
Naidoe aho	go far away
Wesakaput pioneke	The long grass moves
Pek leget tiko oe aho	in the wind
Agomoa silu eke	The grass is bent
Makmagot tike oe aho	downwards in the wind

April 21, 1961

RG to Brew

We have had no mail since arriving three weeks ago today. Yet we know that mail sacks are sitting in Hollandia waiting for someone to remember they should be put on a plane for Wamena. I urge you to send cables to convey any urgent or even semi-urgent information. Even though everyone in North Central New Guinea will know what is said, since it is broadcast in the regular radio frequencies, I will at least hear it in time to act as required.

Everyone is well and extremely busy. Peter is started on his book and seems vastly excited by this place. Mike takes his sound recording very seriously and has more projects than he can ever finish. Karl is apparently happy with his home for the next year or two and has made a good beginning on the language. The filming I have done should fit into the scheme as it slowly evolves. There are some advantages and some disadvantages to this place as against the Kalahari. The advantages include greater objectification or materialization of culture, varied and most often beautiful terrain, limited numbers of people, and the very physical manifestations of the main cultural foci—belligerence toward opposing groups, farming, and pig breeding. Disadvantages include shyness and excessive curiosity about the camera, inability to approach the female aspect of the Dani world, language barrier, humidity problems, and the sheer physical difficulty of walking great distances with heavy loads.

Broekhuyse is a great asset and I am very anxious to persuade the Dutch government to let us use him beyond the time I leave. I have discussed this with Karl, and he is eager that he stay on too. There are many parts of the research he has begun here which he can never hope to finish and which I will need badly later on.

Peter Matthiessen

April 26, 1961

Asch to RG

Your two film shipments arrived yesterday. John or I or Professor Brew will cable you immediately after we have looked at your 29 rolls in work-print.

When you have a moment, be clear about what you would like us to tell and not to tell the press, as there is quite a bit of press around and they are eager for information.

April 27, 1961	**RG's camera notes**

Funeral of warrior—an incredible afternoon—the shots were made on the Filmo since there was no chance of getting among 300 wailing men, women, and children with anything more distressing—a tripod was out of the question—each crank of the handle was for me if not for them a sort of blasphemy—the litany was baroque, the women with their heads veiled by nets, weeping like Sicilians—the boy in his chair of doom and judgment looked contentedly asleep, rocking with the motion of grieving women pressing around him—the whole human dilemma enacted with bits of prehistory, ancient civilization, and contemporary life all represented. Careful notes were made by Matthiessen and Broekhuyse of the ceremony's development. Rockefeller has the sound. It is extraordinary how close to a Pietà the descent from the chair was—but that was only a single aspect. There was not much time to work in the people who came with us (Aloro, Weyak, Wali, Kurelu, Aplegma etc.).

April 27, 1961	**Rockefeller's sound-recording notes**

At the *sili* where the funeral ceremony was taking place. This is the funeral of Ikiarotmilek, the young (about 24) son of the village *kain,* Yoroik. The monotonous moaning comes in response to a chanted few words from a man or woman. The women gathered closely around the seated dead man are related to the dead man and responsible for most of the moaning.

Quality a lot better than the first *etai* tapes. Occasionally there are disturbances. People moved past me on the path and came through the grass toward me in curiosity. There is a little wind noise and occasionally upsetting cable sound that points up the necessity of taping the cable to something.

The best sound picked up during the ceremony: the mike was placed close to first a woman and then a man who were moaning in loud, wailed words in chorus response to the leader. The woman was old and thin, huddled by the *ebeai* [family house]. Her back was to me and she was utterly absorbed in the abandonment of her grief. I have a picture of this woman in one of my wide-angle shots, including the fire; surely Jan has a shot of her too. The man whose voice is prominent seemed to have been important in the ceremony; he often led the moaning and often loudly sounded his grief. This man becomes the fore-singer; he stands before the enthroned corpse. His name is Witariak; he lives in the *sili.* His voice shakes with grief; as he chanted, tears ran down his cheeks and his hands shook as he raised them occasionally toward the corpse.

63

Arranging the funeral chair

April 28, 1961   **RG's camera notes**

Shots of Wittaia on the Siobara [hill and traditional fighting ground] beginning their celebration of the victory validated by the funeral yesterday. They dance and sing, run down onto the Dokolik [fighting ground]. Scene of Aplegma looking and a pan up to distance. Shots of Wittaia going home. 75 feet shot of rain coming over Siobara (sound recorded of the same storm)—Aplegma runs home past bee tree—women go home hurriedly.

April 29, 1961   **RG's camera notes**

Boys (Uwar, Aplegma, etc.) run past camera on way to Weyak's *kaio*. This *kaio* was ripped down by Wittaia when they discovered that one of their women ran away to Homaklep, Weyak's village. They first set a trap for Weyak, but he miraculously avoided their ambush by spending the time talking with us elsewhere. Boys coming to Weyak's *kaio*—they look at it. Shots of nesting cormorants—nestlings and adults—upriver and downriver. More bird shots. 50 feet of *kaio* rebuilding—reaction shots of Aplegma (Weyak's son). Weyak "cleans" (removes any residue of black magic) the men who worked at the rebuilding, makes a symbolic arrow, puts arrow in *kaio* fire for burning sacred leaves—final shot of leaves, bow, and arrows.

April 29, 1961   **RG to Asch and Marshall**

My plan to do little or no shooting for the first month or six weeks has been knocked into a cocked hat by the events themselves. Things have been happening which I could hardly let go by without at least trying to comprehend them in film. The basic plan as I have worked it out in light of developments is to stick pretty much with one film—a story about these warrior-farmers. I will make up my mind soon, I trust, on how I feel about them and how best to convey these feelings in a film. For now, what I'm doing is restricting the leading partici-pants to certain individuals, so that when there is something to see in this culture I will try to arrange that one of these individuals portrays it. Basically I will work with about four men (Weyak, Jegé Asuk, Aloro, and Hanomoak), four boys (Uwar, Aplegma, Pua, and Pelamo), and three or four other figures such as Polik, Wali, and Kurelu. I am counting on the culture, or rather these individuals, to write the story themselves. I shall try to set up limits within which their own actions and the actual events as they transpire will fit. I will not ask them to act beyond the possibilities their own behavior suggests. In a general way I hope that the film will treat the theme of violence.

I am unsure which filmmaking model was uppermost in my mind as I was shooting and, at the same time, searching for the most compelling and appropriate story to tell. Of course, Nanook as a figure in a landscape crossed my mind frequently, as did the "characters" John Marshall and I

65

rounded out from disparate bits and pieces for **The Hunters.** *That exercise had shown me how easy it was to make a palpable figure out of a composite of fragmentary parts radically separated in time and space. I was also drawn to the anonymous or nameless model of figures that had very much come to life in films such as* **Man of Aran** *and* **Song of Ceylon.** *At some early point, I decided on the immediacy of individuals with names, real names by which they were known to each other. I believe that this decision came out of a hope that by providing names I would be providing more actual and accessible people. I thought this helpful, given how seemingly alien the Dani were with their nakedness and odd adornments.*

May 4, 1961

Asch to RG

Carol and I both feel that your color slides are very exciting. I haven't seen any of the movie film yet, but the impression I get from the slides is that the material you have is going to be even more dramatic—the colorful regalia of the warriors and their seeming preparation for battle is likened in my experience to the wonderful battle scene of Olivier's *Henry V*, where the technology of warfare wasn't so far in advance of what you are seeing now. One of the most impressive things is that some men, who apparently are leaders, are wearing the emblems of their personality with them into battle, in much the same way that Eisenstein's Swiss-German knights wore the emblems of their lineage into battle to fight the Russians in *Alexander Nevsky*. In both cases there is this awesomeness and terrifying countenance which belongs to one personality—the stage is magnificent.

May 6, 1961

RG's camera notes

Found a rock high above Wubarainma near Lokopalek [villages] where Jegé Asuk had gone to cut a piece of *yoli* wood from which he wanted to make a spear. Shooting this has been incredibly difficult owing to Jegé constantly mugging and purposefully screwing up. Somewhere in the shooting I tried to get enough light to expose some enemy bones stuck in the crack of a cave wall. There are stories about Dani cannibalism, a very ritualized variety having to do with insulting the enemy, but I haven't yet gotten good information on this. The sequence ended with Jegé Asuk carrying the spear into Wubarainma. I'm not happy and neither is he.

Get *hiperi* [sweet potato] eating sequence where Weyak gets it from a little girl in the *lisé* [long family house]. Use it to cut with the shots I made of Weyak coming back from an early morning walk. Do many Arri shots of Weyak in and around his *kaio*.

May 6, 1961

RG to Asch

Your cable of May 6th arrived this morning. It was terribly garbled by transmission and translation difficulties, but the burden of it said the following: Roll four Willihiman-Wallalua vignetting [image obscured

Weyak

Victory dancing

around the edges]. I have no more idea than this of what you sent in this message. I have spent the entire morning with Elisofon making a developed strip test of the Bell and Howell. Neither of us can see the slightest vignetting. I enclose the developed strips. Please send me a few frames of the vignetting in question (is it on both original and work-print?). From time to time I will make a foot or so test at the beginning of rolls (lenses to be used and exposure to be used). I will state what roll this is on. You should send this to me (the original) and get the rest of the roll work-printed as usual.

It is sheer hell working at such a distance and under the handi-caps of inadequate communication. From the tests I can only assume you to be incorrect or that something very special went wrong with the equipment (filter ring not screwed in? etc.). At the moment I am pretty low.

May 8, 1961

RG's journal

In the early morning I set out to spend as much of the day as possible with Weyak. He cuts a formidable figure, with his powerful and ath-letic physique. He moves with great economy and grace, while still holding in reserve what must be large amounts of energy and strength. He is not especially tall, perhaps 5'8'' and maybe 150 pounds, yet his frame has the musculature that gives the impression of being taller and heavier than he really is. With his physicality goes a genial dis-position. He thinks quickly but deeply, speaks clearly but not sharply, and is firm and thoughtful. Taken altogether he comes close to being admirable. I sometimes regard him, however, with an uneasiness that his apparent good nature might not prevent him from taking the lives of enemy women and children, should they stray across his path.

May 10–11, 1961

RG's camera notes

Etai—attempts made to relate scene in terms of specific individuals— also tried to do more with women—some slow motion shots—also tried running shots.

I was sometimes experimenting with the camera. All of my film work until New Guinea contained material in which conventional documentary tech-nique periodically gave way to, or at least was joined by, efforts to bring other ways of seeing to bear. One technique that always interested me was a shift in rhythm or pace, an altering of time by its lengthening or, more rarely, shortening. In New Guinea I often put ordinary time into a slow modality, hoping to see something in a new and different way. It did not always work but, especially in my more recent films, I feel that it often does. In the final edit of Dead Birds *I removed some shots in which I had used slow motion, in part because I felt the actuality on the screen was already graphic enough, and otherwise because I lost my nerve.*

May 10, 1961

Rockefeller's sound-recording notes

Etai. My state is one of nervous harassment. The scene of the wildly dancing Kurelu, and Wittaia and Kosi-Alua groups as they moved over the stem of the "L" of the Warabara, was completely beyond my expectations. I was so eager to tape sound, take pictures, and steer clear of Bob's movie camera, whose whereabouts I was not sure of, that I lost my head. The final touch came when someone ran off with the knapsack carrying all my tapes.

Rockefeller recording a victory dance

Later material is better. The clicking sound is that of boys and men shaking their bundles of arrows. The sound is more impressive than much of that of the earlier big *etai* because almost the entire group of 100–200 men are singing together. Then after a brief pause there is the sound of a great body of men yelling—a group had suddenly leapt up from where they had been resting, and run off for more *etai*. This sound is altogether too brief. However, it is monotonous and could be repeated over and over and become an excellent war sound, if I get no more opportunity.

May 12, 1961

RG to Asch

This letter is to announce that Shipment 7 will be taken to Wamena tomorrow. From there it is flown to Hollandia, and from Hollandia transshipped to the U.S. Since we are having such a terrific time getting anything from or to Wamena, I have no idea when it will arrive. Letters are sometimes taken out by the missionary Cessna, so they get on their way, but parcels wait for the Dakota, and that can be as long as three weeks.

My biggest worry is exposure. Skins here in average light never give more than 75–100 foot lamberts, whereas the indescribably beautiful skies are from 800–1600. This is due mainly to the high altitude clarity of the air. I honestly don't know half the time what F-stop to shoot at, and there is no chance to bracket half the material [shoot the same subject at more than one exposure] since it is all unique action. Poor Elisofon is going mad and bracketing by a stop and a half on both sides. The next major worry is whether I am getting away with handholding as much as I have had to do. It is one thing to handhold close action with a wide-angle lens and quite another to try the same thing with distant action and a 90mm lens. However, there have been frequent occasions when tripods were either not in camp or utterly impractical. At such times I have had to walk two or three miles, much of it swamp to my crotch, carrying loaded Arri, battery belt, shoulder pod, spare magazine, variable speed motor, extra lenses, light meter, and other necessaries not even associated with photography. I'm afraid even if the situation permitted using a tripod, my stamina would not.

There are a few places on the rolls being shipped where there were camera jams and the door had to be opened to straighten the mess out. Be on the watch for them to take out when looking through the original and assembling it for the printer. I don't know—maybe some whole rolls jumped the registration pin and got dragged past the pressure plate without my knowing it—these are the sort of thoughts I have to live with.

It is now very late at night and there is an early start to make in the morning. Give my best to everyone.

May 16–17, 1961

RG's camera notes

75-foot sequence of Uwar coming past bee tree crying because of eye wound from grass spear—sequence continues to Wubarainma. Jegé Asuk leaves Wubarainma with comrade and with spear—goes toward gardens—sequence of him walking but breaks suddenly as he goes off unwilling to be photographed further.

On May 16th I wrote in my journal the following brief entry concerning the police, who were visiting neighboring villages owing in large part to the complaints of missionaries.

May 16, 1961

RG's journal

Since the visit five days ago by the police inspector and his squad of armed men, all aggressiveness seems to have fled the Willihiman-Wallalua. They are still manning their watchtowers and are still afraid of the ghosts of slain enemy warriors, but I detect an apathetic population. It may be a long wait until the next battle.

I was beginning to wonder whether the pattern of ritual warfare was going to change and I would be left having to think of a different focus for the film. I was already committed to the theme of human aggressiveness and had no wish to alter my plan to pursue this theme wherever it took me. Still, the situation was delicate. We were promised independence, and yet, although the whole world was not watching, a small and vocal part of it— including missionaries and reporters—was. An example of our problem was the need to keep closely held the intelligence that Michael was grazed in the leg by an arrow in a battle at about this time. Were it to become known, all parties to our presence among the Dani would have had differ- ent ways of explaining it, and different reasons for explaining it—with unpredictable consequences for our work.

May 18, 1961

RG to Marshall

I have pretty much decided on making only one film; at least, that is all I am working on at present. When the material for it is in hand, I will turn to one or possibly two others, a film on the salt trade and a film on the Baliem River itself. For the present film I have selected about ten major characters: four boys, four youngish men, and two or three older men. One of my boys has already gone over the horizon,

Watching for the enemy

thinking I was going to beat him for taking my knife. I have tried to make all the action take place in the presence of these individuals. There has been very little direction as far as having them do anything is concerned, but quite a lot as far as having them in on what I'm doing is concerned. You will see some of my painful experiences trying to get sequences, though I will say that as "actors" they are far better than the Bushmen.

In the first batches of film I sent back there were a great many photographic attempts at providing transition, i.e., swing pans (blurred pans to sky to trees to anything), the idea being that I would cut from one middle of a swing pan to another middle. You might tell me what you think of this idea and also whether the pans are enough in the right direction vis-à-vis each other and enough the right speed to cut together.

Recently I have been making considerable use of a very consistent feature of all these people's lives, which is a tremendous gift to me as an editor, and that is their constant looking out over the fields or hills or trees or anywhere. I have been making quite a few shots of people just looking up, or looking in various directions. They do this because they are continually alert for their enemy sneaking up to swipe a pig or something. I also want to use animals a great deal, and have been experimenting with various small creatures found around and about.

As yet I cannot put down a blocked-out screen treatment, partly because it is not entirely thought out and partly because I don't want to freeze it just yet. I do want to take advantage of the splendid terrain here and have a film in which viewers are secure in knowing where they are at all times. You will notice that I have used the Warabara as a terrain feature—it is the focal natural formation of the whole film, a small hill out in front of these people. Their lives are led all around it, and some are lost upon it. There is a mountain behind our camp which I have strained my gut climbing on with the Arri to make pictures of the various important landmarks. I would like to know whether these are clear, what more should be done to orient the spectator, and so forth.

I work completely alone on this thing and have had to carry everything long distances. My camera notes, written in the evening after much is already forgotten, are thus not complete. When the rolls are printed you can simply look back at these notes for a skeleton explanation of what is happening. Your comments will revive my memory and serve to tell me where I have succeeded and failed.

This letter to John Marshall was an attempt to connect with another film-maker as I worked at various strategies with the Dani. It also indicates further commitment on my part to the subject and style I had decided to pursue. It may come as close as anyone in my situation would want to come to disclosing their artistic intentions.

Pua with his pigs in the early morning

The following entry in my camera log tells of the choice I had definitively made of Pua as the principal child personage for the film. I made this choice for the reasons stated: I remember wanting a child who was not in the tradition of slick Hollywood brats but one who could represent the frailty and vulnerability I thought so necessary to my emerging story.

May 18–20, 1961 **RG's camera notes**

Pua sequence. Pua is one of the three or four little boys I am concentrating on. He is the smallest and most ungainly, flat headed and round bellied, but also the most endearing. Sequence has to do with his activities in the morning as a youthful swineherd. The action takes place in the abandoned gardens in front of our camp, which are used by various families as places to fatten pigs. Shots of Pua with Warabara behind him. Many shots of bees and other bugs fertilizing old *hiperi* blossoms. Shots of boys beginning to fight a little. Pua does some herding partly because he must and partly because he is not a good fighter. Boys start a small-scale war with grass spears and arrows. Pua starts home with pigs.

May 24, 1961 **RG's journal**

The last several days have passed amid hope, despair, and finally certainty that normal life would resume among the Willihiman-Wallalua. On the 11th of May a police patrol made a visit to our neighborhood. On several subsequent days, patrols were sent to warn warriors that, if they fought any more, they would be taken off to jail in Wamena.

When I went to Wamena on Friday, I met with Broekhuyse, who had gone there to visit his wife and child prior to their departure for the Netherlands. He told me he had been called to Hollandia to answer charges based on fictitious accounts of his activities put out by both Protestant and Roman Catholic missionaries. I decided to go to Hollandia myself to try and straighten the matter out.

My thinking on the problem confronting us dwelled mostly on ways to restore our independence. A number of factors had to be taken into consideration. Above all were the verbal guarantees by the Dutch that we would be unmolested by police or other visitors. On the other hand, an allegation had been put forward by the local government in Wamena that our toleration of warfare was leading to new outbreaks of violence in the valley.

The problems stirred by our not entirely dispassionate study of Dani culture, including of course their ritual warfare, tend to heighten the basic anxiety of officialdom that the internal situation might not appear to the outside world as entirely settled and humane. That there is ritual war in the Baliem Valley is something all people who have lived in that valley know for a certainty; but what no one has bothered to find out is what warfare means to those who make it or what it could mean to deprive them of it.

Following discussions with various government figures in Hollandia, I returned to the Baliem Valley where another conference took place with the local authorities.

In this last set of conversations with government representatives, we were able to find a harmonious way to keep working in our accustomed manner and also to shield local government officials from embarrassing political or missionary accusations that we were fomenting discord in the valley. The solution was to have the local authorities disclaim jurisdiction over the part of the Baliem Valley in which we worked. That area, called Kurelu, had already been designated "unpatrolled and uncontrolled," and this status was made clearer to all concerned.

May 26, 1961 — **RG's camera notes**

Two rolls of *weem* on the Warabara. This is the most intense battling yet—things happened much too fast to remember or write down—concentration was on engagement, particularly with spears.

May 26, 1961 — **Rockefeller's sound-recording notes**

The battle begins again, this time reaching a new height—frantic yelling of instructions—the rise and fall of the yelling. The wildest moment of all came with the culminating drive by the Wittaia. They swept our warriors entirely off the Warabara. For a moment before running myself, I taped the warriors as they streamed past me. The end of the tape is qualitatively the best sound. Marvelous whooping between the two sides with a terrific take of singing that goes on as the battle dies down at one point.

May 27, 1961 — **RG's camera notes**

At the *etai*, where there were *sué warek* ["dead birds" or "dead men," the captured enemy arms and decorations]. Most of the material is of the end, including a short sequence of the dead birds being carried off by the war leader Nilik.

May 27, 1961 — **Rockefeller's sound-recording notes**

The sound of the circle of important figures discussing the "dead birds." I was trying to anticipate some ceremony connected to the magnificent pole of "dead birds" before the *etai* hut. Nilik just got up, undid the spears and arrows, and took them off.

On April 9, 1961, I wrote the following lines in my journal: "When these men kill an enemy, they take his ornaments, feathers, weapons and any other possessions the victim may be carrying. These are called dead birds (sué warek), a term that refers, almost interchangeably, to dead men."

Matthiessen and Gardner close to the skirmish line

Dead birds *(sué warek)* on display at an *etai*

By this time in our stay with the Dani, I was thinking about how they handled thoughts about their own mortality and how their ritualization of warfare played a part in this thinking. I am not sure that the title Dead Birds *had yet occurred to me, but I do remember dwelling on the happy coincidence of feathers, colored mud decorating weapons, and bloodshed that permeated the scene in front of me.*

May 27, 1961

RG's journal

Exactly ten days ago [the war leader] Husuk came to see me on his way to tell Wereklowé [another war leader] that war was starting on a distant front, breathless for the first time I can remember. Yesterday the Willihiman-Wallalua and some Kosi-Alua fought a savage fight on the Warabara.

May 29, 1961

RG's journal

Broekhuyse and I went early this morning to Weyak's *honai*. He had invited us to come to be with him before the victory celebration that starts later in the day. Weyak is a quiet and considerate man who, though he is without great wealth, commands respect. His age is difficult to guess, but I think he is about thirty-five. Perhaps we were born in the same year.

In his *honai* with us were several men. We spent half an hour talking and smoking while others were eating their morning sweet potatoes. We had brought a Coleman lamp, so I decided to film this quiet interlude. Weyak is utterly considerate, friendly, and maybe most amenable of all the Dani men to the requirements of cinema. He never tires of doing as I ask and I never have to tell him to disregard the camera.

I decided today that Homaklep [Weyak's village] would be a good place to stay a while. Our camp and its routines are confining and too much time is taken up going there for meals, listening to the radio for telegrams, and writing notes at night. Such things should be done, but I also must have the experience of living in direct contact over a period of time with people in their own surroundings.

Such visits to local villages were infrequent overnights that gave an understanding of Dani life available to us in no other way. We all made them, but none of us made the decision to move into a village or a family's house for any extended length of time. This might have been a mistake.

May 31, 1961

RG's camera notes [on filming young boys playing a war game]

Seeds [araucaria] represent armies of men and they are moved around. Sticks are the spears and the boys try to make a hole in the opponent's seed-men. When one does, the "dead man" is carried off to a little pile of other victims. A blind boy plays by himself. Last part is the *kaio* game, where a forked stick is used for a *kaio* and a seed is put up in it. Several shots of the *kaio* against the sky and against the

79

Boys play at war using seeds as men

Gardner, Rockefeller, and Matthiessen watch
boys play at war

Warabara—last shot is of boys getting up and running away down the hill toward their pigs.

Having worked through the problems related to our project being criticized by the missionaries and a few politicians in The Hague, I thought I should write to an official in Hollandia named Rafael den Haan, with whom I had come to an understanding that allowed us to proceed independently to finish what we had started.

June 1, 1961

RG to Rafael den Haan, Commissioner of the Highlands

I would like to thank you for all the time and effort you have put into solving the problems which confronted this expedition only a week ago. It is of the utmost importance, as I am sure you already know, that we be given as complete privacy and isolation as possible. The fact that we can look forward to the remaining months without any non-native activity, except missionaries, among the groups we are studying, is the best assurance possible that our efforts to understand more than is now known of Dani culture will succeed.

All of us are well and working very hard. Mr. Rockefeller is taking a few weeks interruption in the Asmat starting in two weeks but will be back before the end of July.

June 3, 1961

Rockefeller's sound-recording notes

Two men singing as they work with heavy digging sticks. The thumping is that of a digging stick being driven into the ground in order to loosen it in preparation for the planting of potatoes (this scene well developed with photographs). Planting to be done by the women. The men only involve themselves in the heaviest form of gardening such as the rough work in the preparation of a new garden, here a garden which had been allowed to lie fallow for a year or two and was being pressed back into use. They hum an *etai* tune as they work.

June 4, 1961

Rockefeller's sound-recording notes

Whooping. Consternation over Wittaia burning of Wali's *olea* [shelter at the foot of a watch tower]. When I arrived at the *olea*, warriors were re-gathering from the counter attack, which chased the Wittaia out of Willihiman-Wallalua territory. It was during this that Jegé Asuk was wounded. Wali was there, excited and indignant. I immediately set up the tape recorder, sticking my mike hand grip into a *hiperi* dirt mound. I left it alone both to avoid attracting attention to the recording process and to take pictures.

By the beginning of June we were privy to more and more information provided by our growing cadre of mostly young males, and so when a war was in the offing I would sometimes know it far enough in advance to decide what to do. In this first week of June, everyone knew that fighting was not going to be discouraged by patrols, but we worried that nothing was certain and so always went to the scene whenever a battle began.

June 5–6, 1961

RG's camera notes

War started at 1:30 or 2 p.m.—made shots of Weyak leaving Homaklep going to Anelerak [ridge], across the gardens toward Hellerabet [a major *kaio*], past a burning *kaio* shelter, then toward some Kosi-Alua. Did *kaios* and shots of Wittaia challenging. Rain interrupts—men huddle against the wet and cold—shots of Hanomoak, Woluklek, Wali. The fighting never really started—men go home in the rain.

Walking shots up to the Anelerak of Jegé Asuk, where he went to get some sun two days after his arrow wound in the back. He has four or five patches on his front side where he was bled, also a curious needle hole in the vein of his left arm (bled here too?).

Do shots of *nyeraken aré* [cowrie shell strings] being made, as a sort of time symbol—the thread woven by the hand and dropped and woven again and dropped, etc.

Tell Michael to get sound of wind in the banana trees, the rustling of the huge leaves—also belching after eating *hiperi*.

Uwar—do close-ups of *munika* [araucaria seed] spearing.

Wali's *olea,* burned by the enemy

Pua—follow him herding pigs to Alima from high above Wubarainma—get him asleep among the *hiperi* blossoms.

Weyak—close-up of drinking at the Aikhé and close-up of planting his spear in the bank—also climbing *kaio*, sitting in *kaio*, getting down from *kaio*. Material of Weyak in the *lisé* with his family.

One pictorial theme should be the green peace in a landscape that contains not only serenity but murder.

Scene of people bringing wood down from the hills past Pua's pig sty (useful for anticipating a funeral).

Hanomoak dressing his hair, shows his very white teeth in wide smiles.

June 7, 1961

RG's journal

A good night for sleeping. Milika in tent at 6:00 a.m. to speak about his shell—Peter back from Homaklep before breakfast. 30 minutes with Milika, whose legs tremble at the sight of *mikak*. I sit for 15 minutes looking at the valley through binoculars. Suddenly, as if someone had switched on a movie, the whole community of people and places came to life. War on the Dokolik—Peter and I in the swamps and up in the *sien* tree—too hot for heaviest kind of fighting—no bad wounds—another exhausting day.

June 7, 1961

RG's camera notes

Weem. Whole reel shot from *sien* tree by Dokolik (noticed considerable emulsion shavings after changing the magazine—I think it is due to this roll being of slightly greater than standard width)—the tree exactly between the two fronts during the early part of the battle. 300′ taken from swamp on west side of Dokolik (many shots felt shaky—all were handheld as nearly every foot on war has had to be).

At this midpoint of our time with the Dani, the presence of ritual war as a staple fact of their lives was entirely evident. What was less clear was the mechanism of customary thoughts and actions that brought on these clashes. We learned, especially through questions asked by Jan Broekhuyse of Abututi, using a mixture of Malay and Dani, that religious sanctions were the main factors. War was required to redress an imbalance caused by a recent killing between warring groups, and the rules of engagement rested in magical beliefs and ceremonial practices in the hands of important male elders. Frequency of battle seemed more subject to chance than to anything like a fixed schedule, and it was a combination of circumstance and chance, including the weather and ardor for fighting, that determined the number of dead on the field, or those who would die later of their wounds. My efforts to elicit feelings on the part of the warriors themselves were seldom successful, and inquiry usually ended by my being told, "This is our custom."

Rockefeller's sound-recording notes

Taken at the Libarek about 10 a.m.—there I found important *kains* gathered—their soft, furtive conversation before the imminent battle was marvelous. They spoke huddled closely over a small fire. There is an extraordinary amount of teeth grinding. Then the great burst of discussion as the most important *kain* suddenly stood up and ordered the men off to battle.

The sound of the men running in groups of 80 to 150 to and from the battle. The great *kains* yell directions to the forward *kaio* and beyond.

The beginning of the empty sensation of evening on its way. There is a casualness in the air which breeds the feeling among the Willihiman-Wallalua that the Wittaia are no longer a threat. Then several outbursts of taunting, the Willihiman-Wallalua and Kosi-Alua jeering at the Wittaia—a similar display had brought the Wittaia to the devastating attack in the last war.

June 8, 1961 **RG to Asch**

No major problems. I lost the only Series VIII #85 filter I had when crossing an irrigation ditch. But Matthiessen lost a front tooth doing the same thing. He can't eat very well.

I am getting a much better feel of the culture and the individuals I'm working with. Weyak is assuming more and more importance in the scheme of things, partly because he is such a nice guy and partly because he responds so well and so willingly to what I ask. There is another figure I like very much, Woluklek. In a sense I am trying to contrast the two. One is confident and competent as a father, warrior, and farmer. The other is more a dreamer, shy and perhaps even a little frightened. The boys are turning out to be quite hard to work with because they are busy at various chores all the time and I never seem able to convene the ones I want at the same time.

We are pretty well past the midpoint now, and I confess that my thoughts turn more and more in the direction of Cambridge. It is hard to say when we will be finished, but I can assure you that as soon as I feel we are, I will be on my way. This is a very hard country to work in. Communications and transportation are haphazard, and we have come in for more than a full portion of harassment from rather stupid officials and missionaries. It is lucky that I took the time I did to try and take everything with us, because we would have found nothing here, and getting stuff from you takes a tremendously long time, five or six weeks for the lenses, and I still have not gotten the film I wrote for on April 17th.

June 11, 1961 **RG's camera notes**

A boy was speared by the Wittaia at the Aikhé River about 2 p.m. yesterday. His name was Weaké and he had gone with two other boys

Weaké in his funeral chair

Gardner filming the sacrifice of pigs

and a man to drink. The Wittaia were in ambush there, having come in when they saw that Weyak's *kaio* was unmanned (he was at the *wam kanekhé*, ironically the ceremony of strengthening the holy stones for war and general health). Weaké had a wound in his foot and so could not run away fast enough when the Wittaia sprang at the innocent group. He was carried back to Abulapak [Dani compound] when left for dead, bathed in an icy stream to dull his pain, and carried to his *honai* to die at about 6 p.m. Today the funeral took place—shots of his chair—shots of his coming out of the *honai* in his uncle Asikanilep's arms—shots of being put into the chair—shots of funeral and women and mourning—preparation of pig for feast—making *haksé* [cooking pit] and fire for heating stones. Shots of Milika, Polik, Weyak, and Wereklowé (Weyak has very worried expression as he has been blamed for the death). 1:30 p.m.—children feast on ferns (they are prominent at this ceremony). Missed the boy (Weaké) being carried to fire by the perhaps cruel justice of having to change film magazines. Shot of boy on flames—smoke pouring over people—vast crying by all present.

June 10–11, 1961

Rockefeller's sound-recording notes

Important—I have on tape the sound of an old man bringing the news of the death of the small boy Weaké. The old man announcing the death—10 seconds—is great; you can feel the death in his voice. The funeral mourning—the sound is eerie, distant, and empty-like. Then women mourning—all are caught up in the pulse of the elegy—sounds really like a "dying wind." I left the mike untouched on the roof of the *ebeai*—I felt that one half hour of uninterrupted sound might reveal sequences more objectively than otherwise.

Looking back, this notation has a tragic irony. The words Michael recorded when the man told him of Weaké's death were these: "The Aikhé [a river] has eaten him, it has eaten him." That is what would happen about five months later to Michael himself, when he was "eaten" by the Arafoera Sea.

June 12, 1961

RG's camera notes

Wam kanekhé ceremony. After cleaning the holy stones with pig's blood men emerge to clear a path in the straw in front of the *honai* for the *mokats* [ghosts] of the dead warriors to find their way easily to the fronts, where they can do some good for the living warriors. Follow shots of men and boys as they go out to hunt down mice which will be eaten ritually in order to lift the taboo that has been contracted through so much and such close association with holy objects. Many shots of mice hunting.

Shift to *sili* of Weaké's funeral—shots of woman fishing bones from fire—shots of girls with amputated fingers.

Shift to *wam kanekhé* and boys butchering rats and mice—rodents being singed on funeral-like pyre.

High-speed roll used inside the *honai* for the *wam kanekhé* and inside the *lisé* at the ceremony for Weaké—the batteries (nickel cads) for the lights were very old and without much juice and so the light they gave kept failing and growing yellow—maybe there is something anyway.

June 15, 1961   **RG's camera notes**

Shot ducks flying past Weyak's *kaio* (Jegé Asuk shoots a foot or two with my camera without asking to).

June 16, 1961   **RG's camera notes**

Shot of two men greeting a third on ridge (a child at my elbow took hold of the tripod handle and started to move it at the crucial instant—one of the infinite frustrations of this work). 25′ of a man working in a ditch in his garden. Zoom shots of fire that had been lit on spot where Weaké was killed (each afternoon since he was killed a fire has been kindled at this spot).

My camera log entries indicate with increasing frequency that the filming I was doing at this time was directly concerned with something close to a working scheme or outline of wanted shots and sequences. There is far less filmmaking of a scattered or casual kind. Instead, it is now focused on events and behavior springing from a growing sense of coherence and shape in what I was experiencing: events and actions related to violence and death, and the rituals surrounding them.

Despite the lag between sending and receiving messages in almost any form, my connection to John Marshall and Tim Asch, who were working on their own films in Cambridge, was vital.

June 19, 1961   **Marshall to RG**

I think the panning technique may pay off, but some of the pans do not end well—the camera jiggles. In general, I would say that the quick pans, connected with a dissolve between them or even cut directly in the moment of blur, might be the most successful.

The looking out over the country is going to be good—a very successful device.

A general remark: I would *hold longer* on shots that you feel are important. A tendency to clip shots appears throughout the material. Sometimes people do not get out of the frame before the shot ends.

June 21, 1961   **RG's journal**

The rain continues and there are no flights. I used the day trying to sketch the film. The coverage seems vast and sometimes the scale feels appropriately epic. But more material with a little humor and common appeal would help to balance the spectacular. Pua looms more and more important as a sympathetic figure and counterweight to the heaviness of death and misfortune. I want to do closer work with pigs, holy stones, and sacred practice of all kinds. Everything is tied together somehow.

June 22, 1961

RG's camera notes

Pua going to pig sty—he is late and his pigs are ahead of him—looks at himself in puddle—goes to fence and looks out into field, and at this instant cries of war start. Aloro going to front—changes spear for bow and arrow. Fighting at front—men on ridge fighting—Kosi-Alua ambush springs trap and gang surges forward—Wittaia in rout. At this moment the cable in my Arri battery shorted and I was completely without success in starting it up again—with three fresh magazines on my back I had to retreat in humiliation to the rear, where I could pick up the Filmo—by the time I was back the Willihiman-Wallalua had completely routed the Wittaia and they had gone home.

Four rolls shot of operation on and subsequent carrying away of a man called Ekenbuka (means a certain kind of leaf, actually the same leaf used to staunch the blood of his wounds). Both Aloro and Tekman Biok operated on him. Tekman Biok was the one who finally pulled out the arrow which was lodged in his right chest high up, about two inches below the collar bone. It stuck all the way through and was imbedded in his scapula. When Tekman Biok finally got it out the dislodgement sounded like a tub being given one sharp rap with a rubber hammer. Uwar was on the edges of this event. Very rapidly done with Filmo in fading light.

June 26, 1961

Asch to RG

Three days ago I was winding the Shipment 10 original onto cores to be sent to Color Service for work-print and noticed several bad scratches. I phoned John, who verified this. He thought it would be best to fly to New York immediately. I got through several more rolls and noticed the same kind of scratches, and at 12:30 at night phoned the airlines and made a reservation for the next morning. To make a long story short, they have admitted that the scratching was done during processing, as they admitted the same on an earlier roll of film. All of this certainly doesn't inspire confidence in the work Kodak is doing. I will tell you what you have to shoot again as soon as I find out by looking at the work-print. Actually, Eastman doesn't bother me now nearly as much as does the lack of confidence I have developed in my inspection of Color Service labs ...

These people all now know, if they didn't before—and I don't really think that they cared as much before—that this film is in a way a national treasure, that it is invaluable, and that there are an awful lot of people who are concerned with what's being done with it.

Do not be disheartened by this tale. I write it mainly to let you know that we are doing the very best we can for you. You've taken an awful lot of film besides these problematic rolls, and an awful lot

Letting a wounded man's blood

of it is really superb. I would like to say that I think the more close-ups the better. By and large, the exposure could not be any better than it is, and you were right in using the Ektachrome Commercial film that you took with you.

June 28, 1961

RG's camera notes

Nine rolls of the women's salt-well journey—I purposefully shot almost all scenes of party going to the wells from behind and nearly all scenes of the party returning from in front.

June 28, 1961

RG to Asch

I have received and answered the telegram you sent on the 20th. I was actually up on a hill behind the camp early in the morning trying to do some stop motion photography of a lovely mist-rising dawn when I heard the sleepy voice of the Wamena radio operator beginning to repeat the letters in the words of your telegram. As far as the whole message was concerned, there was no way to know just what was in it until I got down to Wamena last Friday, since Karl and the others were not able to make it out either, what with the reception and pronunciation.

I got your thought in the telegram about the need for close-up material. I don't know from the telegram where this material is needed, but I assume it must be in the funeral. At this funeral, without actually asking people to move, there was practically no place to stand, let alone get a decent film shot. Everyone was at temper's end about our being there, so there were many figurative toes stepped on. They would let only me take a camera, and our friends kept trying to put me into a house where no one would bother to spear me. If there is anything on this funeral, it is a plus, and since there was another one recently in a village we know quite well, I think the subject is fairly covered.

I have reached the conclusion that I cannot do without seeing the material myself—which does not mean that I don't want your notes too. It takes roughly two months from the time I send you film, to hear what is on it, and if I go to Japan I will only see a part of the trip's work. Please don't interpret anything I have said as more than frustration and, I may say, a growing loneliness. In two months, or even less, I will feel that I have spent more than enough time on the photography of one film.

The talks with den Haan and other Dutch officials weeks earlier finally resulted in an acknowledgement duly recorded in official proceedings:

July 1, 1961

Proceedings of the New Guinea Council, Hollandia

Information has been received by rumors, about the activities of the American film expedition operating in the Baliem, by the Honorable Deputies Father Van de Berg and Dr. Kamma. It was requested by Dr.

Kamma that vague rumors, difficult to control, be brought into their true proportions. The government agreed to do this. This concerns the film expedition of the Harvard Peabody Museum which, under the direction of Mr. Robert Gardner, Director of the Harvard Film Study Center in Cambridge, U.S.A., is making a scientifically justified ethnological film of some local Dani groups in an ungoverned part of the Baliem.

Father Van de Berg thought that in the region where the expedition is operating, the waging of war had been permitted by the authorities in order to allow the expedition to film it, which would cause confusion among other Dani groups. The government insists on clarifying that the territory where the expedition is active, is an ungoverned part which has remained thus far outside the boundaries of the actual exertions of the local government. In such regions there is no interference in small tribal wars unless such happenings are a menace to the established order and peace of a neighboring governed territory. The government is of the opinion that this certainly is not so in this case, and therefore does not see any reason to withdraw the permit of residence of this expedition for the concerned territory. This matter has been thoroughly discussed with the leader of the expedition.

Moreover, rumors which speak of the provocation to acts of war by members of the expedition, appear to be—after a careful study—entirely untrue.

July 2, 1961

RG to Marshall

I know that if there is anyone who understands the predicament I'm in, it is you—away from what you most need, the film on a screen, and waiting on the most inadequate system of communication yet called a system (and permitted to operate as such) to tell you something—anything—and then when something comes it is never enough.

I am interested in your comments about the shortness of scenes and the clipped quality to some of the shots. In many situations I have been shooting under tense conditions, and my reaction was to do as little camera pointing as possible, or shall I say, as much camera pointing for as short a time as possible. The unconscious plan may have been to get as much on film as possible—I also have the feeling that I should economize on film, and so I have been trying to cram. Also, I have had a lot of trouble controlling the people variable—these people are not actively hostile to pictures being made, but they are often rather nasty and muggish when they see me doing it. Some latent wisdom tells them that they will screw me, if they stick their tongues out. Also, I have used the extreme wide-angle lens quite a lot, and that has meant that the action is seen for a long time, often longer than the spring in the Filmo lasts—and people are still not out of frame. I am going to start using the 25mm lens more, and I think this will help.

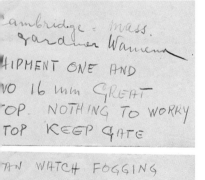

A note from John Marshall

As of now just about everything has happened that I could ask for (though when I asked to film the birth of a child and the man said ok, I went when called about three miles up into the cloud wet mountains at six in the morning to discover the child had been born while I was on the way). There have been two funerals since that first one of the young man—one a small boy speared to death ten minutes from my tent, and then yesterday an ancient man with whom I did some work earlier, thinking he had very little time left.

Since my recent talks with the government, police action has stopped in this area, as it should have always been since it is an uncontrolled area, and the warriors are not being intimidated. I trust there will be a few more encounters in which I can do some special work on individuals before I have to leave. When we leave, the government is sending in a force to stop war in this, one of the last areas of traditional hostilities.

I hope all your work is going well. I envy you the use of a screen. I would say this is the last time I will try a film without using a projector in the field, if I didn't feel pretty sure that this is the last time, period. I feel the separation from life and people pretty severely.

July 4, 1961

RG's camera notes

Shots of a man being carried back from Warabara after a Wittaia ambush—shots of Uwar and another boy reacting to the dead man—a warrior fires *lokop* [type of grass] arrows over corpse—corpse is smeared with pig blood—shots of litter being carried off toward Abulapak.

July 5, 1961

RG's camera notes

Shots of men sneaking along Aikhé—very distant shots of battle far out on the swamp beyond Warabara—shots of wounded being brought back—shots of women waiting for the dead.

July 8, 1961

RG to Asch

I sent the following telegram to you yesterday: AIR EXPRESS ALL WORKPRINT TO ME CARE DEBRUYN OFFICE OF NATIVE AFFAIRS HOLLANDIA STOP SEND FIFTY ROLLS ONE HUNDRED FEET EKTACHROME COMMERCIAL STOP STILL NEED FILTERS. As for the Hollandia screening, I have decided I could do it faster and cheaper there than Tokyo, and I will take my chances on the government not interfering. I don't think they will, because we have reached a very good and pleasant understanding about all matters relating to our work.

I hope you realize it was never my intention to make your life miserable. I know what it is like to do what you are doing, because it is what I did for John when he went to Africa the last time. Shipments of film were coming in and going out all the time, and stuff was being requisitioned by telegram a mile a minute. No matter

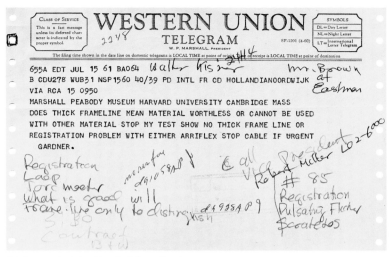

A telegram to John Marshall from Gardner

how carefully one tries in planning this kind of an operation, things are forgotten or things are in short supply or something goes wrong.

What I have missed sorely is a shot-by-shot rundown—I appreciate John's notes on viewing the film, but the remarks, no matter how cogent in a general sense, fail to provide the sort of information that I need to retake or develop certain lines. Until recently I thought of sending a continuity I have made giving the roll numbers and approximate positions within the roll of the shots I would like to use. However, I realize that it would be a stupendous chore for anyone such as yourself to undertake to see if the shots I have indicated are present and if they are, whether they are sufficient unto the demands of the continuity—it would not only take much too much time, but it would take an appreciation of the film that obviously only I can supply. Instead, I have decided to see all I can of the work-print myself and whether the knowledge of what there is will sustain and inspire me to the end, perhaps another month.

It is lucky I took four cameras, because one Arri is not so hot, with broken cable connector, and one of the Filmos is pretty sick with turret trouble. The most trouble technically that I have been having lately is poor contact with the cable connection to the camera—the very high humidity here is beginning to take its toll—cables get corroded.

July 13, 1961

Letter to Asch continues

Tuesday I got cables obscure enough in meaning and seemingly urgent enough to warrant an attempt to get down the river to Wamena. Broekhuyse and I set forth, and in trying to get the boat over a log, we capsized. Broekhuyse almost drowned, and the motor went to the bottom. We got the motor out and walked home four miles through a bamboo thicket and swamp. Yesterday we came back to raise the boat, and Karl and I paddled eight hours to Wamena, chopping our way through trees and branches exposed by low water. We got in last night to hear that the transmitter was being moved and that there would be no regular contact until the morning. I worked on the engine from eight to two and finally got it going. Shipment #13 is on the Dakota, which came in this morning much to everyone's surprise.

From the telegram John just sent it is very hard to know what problem if any exists with the frame line and registration. The strips I have developed show no problem. This is all just part of the mystery I live in constantly.

July 17, 1961

RG's camera notes

Follow shots of Weyak going up Anelerak—looks out there—goes along to Puakoloba [his *kaio*]—looks momentarily at burned ground where blood of Weaké was scorched—shots inspecting area around *kaio*.

Uwar looks into pool where Weaké was murdered.

July 17, 1961

Rockefeller's sound-recording notes

I had never before attempted to do something specifically with the girls alone, this on account of their shyness and their mothers' and the men's fear as to what I would do with them. But when I suggested that I go with one of them to see the pigs and where they were taken, I met with only transient objection. The pigs were left to graze by the Elokhera River. Afterwards some girls took me over the mountain, presumably on the way back to the *sien* wood. Here I coaxed them into singing, but only a little bit. They repeatedly said they knew no songs—obviously not true. They sang in Dani, "Mike went to Hollandia. Karl will go to America. I wonder what their mothers will do." The girls picked lice from each other's hair while they sang—it seems as if the Dani rarely sing without doing something else—they sing for functional reasons or while they work.

Women asking Gardner for favors

July 18, 1961

Asch to RG

About your letter of June 28th—how sad it is indeed to learn that even telegrams we have been sending are not received as we hoped they would be. Our last hopes of communicating directly with you have just gone down the drain. I never did get the telegram about what to send with Sam. You are, of necessity, really isolated and frustrated for information, and it is not so much our fault as the fault of an extremely poor communication system.

We saw Shipment 11. The most important film here is that taken of battle (all of which you will see presently), some of it taken from a tree and some from the ground—all of it utterly fantastic photography and situation. However, you have a frame line problem and no one is exactly sure what it is.

A problematic frame line was the last thing I wanted to hear about, and as soon as I was convinced nothing of this nature was amiss I went about pursuing my filmmaking goals. From the time I had decided that Pua would be prominent in the film, I worked with him in as many contexts as I could. Accordingly, I asked Michael to record sound with him as well. I grew ever fonder of Pua as we spent more time together.

July 18, 1961

Rockefeller's sound-recording notes

Pua working in garden and singing "Waliké, Waliké."

July 21, 1961

RG's camera notes

Pua makes a little garden—many shots. Little girl coming with *hiperi* for Pua to eat—shots of Pua eating (he bit into a *hiperi* that was full of worms and kept spitting out the pieces). Sequence of Pua making up his arms and face with yellow clay (he and others related to Yonokma [a warrior killed earlier] are still doing this as a sign of mourning)—runs over to fence to look at hawk sailing above the gardens.

July 23, 1961

RG's camera notes

Pua and bones sequence. Pua paints his eyes—goes to bone rock—shots of him looking at rock—shots of lizard—shots of Pua looking and then suddenly bolting. Shots of Pua playing at throwing dishes of wet clay so they can explode. Shots of Pua herding pigs.

July 23, 1961

RG to Asch and Marshall

I got the fat envelope sent the 23rd of June. The notes were wonderful to get, even though I shall be going down in a few days to see the film myself. You provide exactly the sort of information I need—I get a clear picture of what is on the various rolls.

There has been another very rainy period and consequently a slacking off of activities. I have had a chance to do some setup work, which I am glad for, though even directing the action means difficulties of all kinds. I don't speak fluent Dani by any means and therefore cannot often express what I really want, and even when they do get the idea, the request often strikes them as so ridiculous, the whole thing looks to me pretty wooden.

I figure that if nothing much happens in the next few days, I will have about 10,000 feet to finish with after screening the film and knowing pretty much what I want.

I sit here wondering when the world is going to shake with hydrogen explosions—all hell seems about to be let loose. It is not a happy feeling with everyone I know so far away.

July 26, 1961

RG to Asch

I am busily preparing to leave tomorrow for Wamena and subsequently Hollandia in order to see the work-print. Very little has

95

happened over the past two weeks except rain. I wish the present lull had occurred while I was in Hollandia or as soon as I returned, so that I would not miss anything important and so that I could go straight to work on filling in what I need. Perhaps the lull will continue until we leave—plenty has certainly happened so far.

August 2, 1961

RG's camera notes

Pua sequence in which he leaves Wubarainma because one of the pigs in his care wandered off toward the Aikhé (echo of Weaké).

Tell Michael I need sound of Weyak talking from his *honai* to people in the *lisé* in the early morning—also get responses from the women in the *lisé*.

August 3, 1961

RG's journal

Pua's threat yesterday morning to run away may only be temporarily blunted by my offer of a machete. He is very independent, stubbornly so, and filled with mercurial reactions. He was recently beaten by his stepfather for letting one of his pigs wander too close to the Aikhé. I have now been told the story of Weyak's name, which means "wrong." He is said to have hit his wife hard enough to kill her when he found she had deceived him.

August 6, 1961

RG's camera notes

A man named Asukuwan came to see me at 10 a.m. to get his *wal-imoken* [snail shell ornament] that I had pressed for four nights under my air mattress to flatten it out. He said he was going to war and that I should come along later. At 10:30 I saw Weyak and Asukuwan leave Homaklep and start out across the fields along the western side of the Anelerak so as not to be seen. They crossed the outer fields, stopped briefly at Hellerabet, and continued on to Wali's *kaio,* where they stopped.

August 10, 1961

RG to Asch

I am back from having viewed the work-print. The day after I returned there was war, and about four or five days after that another one. From viewing the work-print I realized that some telephoto material would be good, and so among other chores during these past two encounters I set up with the 150mm on a tripod. I used the 300mm a little in the August 2nd conflict but hated to because the work-print showed me that it is quite soft at infinity. However, I was able to move close enough to focus it fairly critically and perhaps there is something of value in having done so.

The Bell and Howells have been retired, and all I am currently using is the newer Arri. I have noticed no more emulsion shavings since the unfortunate experience in a tree above the battle—an experience I am delighted to have had because of the really remarkable outlook I enjoyed, but which I terribly regret because of the camera trouble involved.

We have all had a look at the still contact sheets you sent with the work-print, and I am quite encouraged by them. They show a falling off in technical aspects, exposure, etc., but a definite gain in pictorial interest. You must remember that many of the blank frames are because the cameras are being handed around, people have forgotten what they shot, and rolls have been rewound before they are fully shot. I think the stills for the rest of the trip are going to be very good, and that with Eliot's stuff and all that has been done by the others there will be quite a fascinating collection.

August 9, 1961

Asch to RG

I am greatly relieved and wonderfully happy to read that you are finally certain you know what you have done and that you think you have a film. John has always been much more optimistic than I, having slipped into a pessimistic train of thought as I continued in my harassed position here in trying to see that you were served as well as possible. We are all hoping that the rest of your venture proceeds with much less pain and anxiety.

August 11, 1961

Rockefeller's sound-recording notes

Weyak—making *nyeraken aré*—good teeth grinding—casual talk—running out of the house—very good pigs and breathing sounds. Then he is inside by a fire—he sings a little. Three men talk in *honai*—interesting with many various "sounds of living"—movements, breathing, sighs, etc.

August 14, 1961

RG's camera notes

The Siobara is like the sun or moon—it seems to follow wherever one goes, so overwhelmingly present is it—it dominates pictorially.

The Siobara

August 15, 1961

RG's camera notes

Noticed difficulty starting a shot—the film was swollen from humidity to the point where it wouldn't pass through the gate! This has to be at the root of the registration problems.

Made close-ups of Pua on hillside, also middle shot from behind to go with lizard shots. Shots of Pua and Okoniké [his mother], then several shots of her and Pua and the *sien* forest (this to tie in with his going off to his mother's brother's family).

August 18, 1961

Asch to RG

I have just looked at Shipment 13 and it really looks excellent, better than anything I have seen before. The shooting seems much more relaxed, and we have a much longer chance to look deeply into the activities of the people you are living with. Perhaps it is only axiomatic to say that in getting close to people there is absolutely no substitute for living with them for a long period of time.

August 21, 1961

RG's camera notes

Shots of Pua taking out pigs—slow-motion of Pua running away from Siobara.

August 22, 1961

RG to Asch

This will probably be the last letter you get from me. It would be dishonest to say that I am sorry about the prospect of leaving quite soon. The last few weeks have been very hard indeed. The camp is full, the food gets worse, rain has poured for ten days, and the "natives" are on top of me every second. I have not bathed, dressed, slept, eaten, or tied my shoes in privacy for almost six months. On top of the usual end-of-expedition fatigue, John's telegram about a "processing fault" came last Friday. Since Shipment 13 is rather key in the whole scheme of things, this news nearly undid me. For the last week I have worked without confidence in my cameras or technique or the destiny of the film material once it leaves my hands.

August 23, 1961

RG's journal

The strain caused by our presence is beginning to tell on us all, especially on me and through me on those I work with most intensively. Pua cries, Wali is in a frenzy of nervous laughter, and Weyak merely looks harried. The knowledge that we are going and the police will be coming is sinking in. We all are living with a deadline and that is affecting everyone.

August 24, 1961

RG's camera notes

Did some shooting of salt burning with Okoniké and Pua. The little mound of ashes reminds me of how easy it is to reduce to almost nothing a tremendous effort, beginning with the gathering of the

Pua's mother rendering salt

materials needed to make salt, and ending with the work of raising a son to be a warrior.

August 25, 1961

RG's journal

Tonight I wanted to film Pua eating a pretty yellow-faced bird. Instead a man was killed, and Pua put his little spear into his lifeless body just the way some others did, symbolically sharing in the homicide

The murder of the man from the enemy side of the frontier was a complex affair. At its root was a general dismay caused by a prolonged period of waiting by those in our midst who wanted to right the balance of deaths that had weighed against them for too long. All the Willihiman-Wallalua were downcast and suffering spiritual decline. Their *etai-eken* (seeds of singing) were in a depleted and sickened state. There had to be a death among their enemy in order to restore their health and vigor.

While I was in the valley, I was once told that a woman who had come to visit her relatives in a Willihiman-Wallalua village was going to be killed. I managed to prevent it from happening, but this man, who seemed to have come across no-man's land to steal a pig, was not so fortunate. He was discovered and cruelly stabbed to death with spears. It was at night, and when word finally reached me, my way to his corpse was lit only by moonlight. It was a troubling sight and added to my growing lack of appetite for violence.

This death was a classic, almost predictable, bit of Dani revenge and retaliation. I wondered if it resonated with revenge in other societies, and I wondered more acutely than ever how the scenes I had shot might be used and whether they would contribute to an understanding of the phenomenon of human violence. The occasion of the murder persuaded me that our inquiry could, even should, come to end, and that we would have to go home to consider the full meaning of what we had been witness to for almost half a year.

August 26, 1961

RG's camera notes

Frog in a ditch—juxtapose with dead Wittaia man in ditch—use frog as substitute for Pua.

Men gathered to dance on the Anelerak—Pua watches quietly—are they feeling guilty at all?

August 27, 1961

RG's camera notes

I shot the trail of blood left when the Witttaia corpse was dragged off toward the Libarek. I also shot the sequence of Pua plucking, cooking, and eating a little bird in his house. The mood is quite somber for us all.

Carrying home a man killed in ambush

A film splicer

shaping the film

Several decades have elapsed from the time of our dispersal as observers in a stone age warrior-farmer community in the highlands of New Guinea and the imprecise moment when Dead Birds, *my completed film, could be said to have moved fully into the film-going universe. An intense period of film editing was followed by the much longer time—to the present moment, in fact—of the film's circulation throughout the world, as it has found its audience and either missed or made its mark on an unnumbered multitude of students and ordinary film watchers.*

The time of the film's shaping brings into this story an expanded cast of characters but includes some from the original team, in particular Peter Matthiessen, Jan Broekhuyse, and Karl Heider. Heider, who stayed among the Dani, reported on the changes there over the next two years resulting from the pacification of the local people and the Indonesian takeover of western New Guinea. Again, letters, logs, and various other documents form the skeleton of the narrative, and my own memories and reflections provide the connective tissue.

We left the Baliem Valley on August 31, 1961. Following a few days in Hollandia, where we closed down our highland enterprise, I returned to Cambridge early in September. Peter had gone back to Long Island after stopping in Australia to repair his broken front teeth, and following a visit to see me and his family in the United States, Michael would return to New Guinea to organize his journey to collect art in the Asmat region. Michael's time with me was short, only a day or two, during which he talked enthusiastically of his forthcoming adventures. We also spoke about the sadness he was feeling about his parents' impending separation and divorce. Like Karl, Jan was still at work in the highlands of New Guinea. Sam Putnam and Eliot Elisofon had returned earlier to their respective lives in medicine and photography.

When I first arrived home, I was ordered to bed with a mysterious ailment provisionally called "sand fly fever." I don't remember many sand flies in New Guinea, but my physician had been an army doctor stationed in New Guinea during World War II and he insisted on his diagnosis. I remember those days as a time when I looked at every color photograph we had made. I think it was clear even in my fevered state that a book should be done to make these photographs known. Michael and I had agreed that this could be one of his responsibilities when his Asmat collecting was finished. Peter was hoping to get his book Under the Mountain Wall *published quickly, and I had many invitations from publishers of both magazines and books for articles and manuscripts. Most importantly, after I shook off the sand fly fevers, I set about preparing for what I knew would be a long siege of filmmaking.*

September 29, 1961 **RG, in Cambridge, to Gerbrands, in Leiden, Netherlands**

As you can see, I am already back in the United States. Mike Rockefeller will have a movie camera in the Asmat during October and November. He will be in Ammanamgai during the latter part of

October. If you want any scenes for your film, write him immediately, c/o HPB, Agats, Netherlands New Guinea. Michael comes back about January 1st. He will have collected art and sound recordings. The latter can, of course, be used in your movie. Also, the Museum of Primitive Art is interested in your work either as a show, publication, or both.

October 4, 1961

Heider, in New Guinea, to RG

All is not the same. They [the Dutch] have established a [police] post fifteen minutes away, towards the Elokhera. Jegé Asuk, who knows where the future lies, has joined. Even Uwar is now a police boy junior class—he has deserted Wubarainma. I can already feel things coming apart at the seams.

It is all very frustrating. I am only able to pick up bits of information. Two days ago there was to be a great gathering—about 50 women and 25 men assembled on the Anelerak. I got to the top of the Turoba and found that the whole thing was called off. Why? I got four different explanations, and I understood none, really.

October 13, 1961

Heider to RG

Today the police held a great peace meeting on the Dokolik. Kurelu was there, apparently in charge. The Wittaia delegation was headed by Watlé (in chains until they were ceremonially removed). I have no idea of how it will come out. Wali talks of rebuilding Likinapma with the Wittaia ... he is on the ground floor as always. So the Pax Hollandia has settled in.

Last week I gave my talk at the Berglands Conference [in Hollandia]. The discussion turned to effects on the Dani of this sort of transition. I am impressed by the way in which everyone laughs at everyone else behind their backs. Of course, now they have more things to think about—will the United Nations arrive before Sukarno?

October 17, 1961

RG to Heider

Just got your October 4th letter. A very distressing picture it is you paint. I did not think the collapse would be as sudden and total as what you describe.

Things jerk along here. There is an immense amount to do and too few to do it.

We can use, in fact we desperately need, color material of a high photographic quality on the following topics: women's labor; child, mother situations; material culture close-ups; *etai* highlights; funeral close-ups.

Next week I start the interminable process of editing the film. I hope there will not be any need of requesting fill-in shots, but I suppose I'll have to. I will send you a rehabilitated Filmo.

Mike was here for a visit and must now be in the Asmat.

October 17, 1961 | **RG to de Bruyn, in Hollandia**

By now, I have seen all the film and all the color slides. There is excellent material in both categories. The black and white negatives are of such vast quantity that we have not even been able to print everything as yet, but from what I have seen I am very pleased indeed.

October 19, 1961 | **Heider to RG**

Our friends and allies are going wild over there on the Elokhera—a great fort with barn (for the police) and two *honais* (for the scabs) wasn't enough to keep the people busy for long, so now they are working on a road. Yes. Presumably to follow the trail of blood to the Dokolik, then who knows—perhaps a tunnel under the swamp, then to Maxey's [missionary post]. I suppose that will allow a plane to taxi in from Tulem. Everybody is working there now—Weyak, Wali … Polik is the foreman. Well, it does give them something to do.

November 2, 1961 | **Heider to RG**

The Great White Way is going to follow the Dokolik, swing around the Sukola, and go to the Baliem near the Aikhé mouth. Then, with the road that far, they will tell Hollandia they need a bridge. There is some sort of expert up from the city to weatherproof the Wamena strip—he plans to blow up a hill and use the rubble for base and cover it with asphalt.

November 15, 1961 | **Heider to RG**

Things get worse and worse. The police have the Dani over a barrel. The only consolation is that when the Indonesians, the U.N., and finally the Papua Barat [Indonesian for "West Papua"] take over, things will be much worse.

But I am just now beginning to feel that my time is being well spent—good stuff coming out every day—a trickle still but solid.

Weyak has cut (or let be cut) his hair so that now he is practically unrecognizable. Wali is the same, but he has been stealing pigs and so hides up in Lokopalek.

Rockefeller in the Asmat

Karl's news from the Baliem Valley was distressing enough, and it made our work even more urgent as the record of a society undergoing rapid and devastating change. Then, on a particular but uncertainly remembered day and hour, I received a call from Governor Nelson Rockefeller's office in New York, telling me that the Netherlands Embassy had just called to inform the governor that his son Michael was missing off the coast of southern New Guinea. I was asked to meet the governor at what was then Idlewild Airport (now JFK) to board a flight departing within hours to Honolulu, where there would be a chartered Boeing 707 ready to take us to New Guinea.

I was at home when the call came, having dinner en famille *with two close friends. It was the age not of credit cards but of traveler's checks, and of course the banks were closed. Luckily the friends who had come for dinner were habitual carriers of large sums of cash. I borrowed what I could, put some things in a bag, and went to the airport for a flight to New York City.*

My memory is that many people were on hand to accompany the governor other than myself, including Michael's twin sister, Mary, Eliot Elisofon (as a Life *photographer), a body guard, several press secretaries, and what must have been a few dozen reporters from newspapers and magazines, some of whom would go only as far as Honolulu and others who would continue to New Guinea.*

This media interest came from Rockefeller's general renown as a politician and multimillionaire, but there was an added frisson arising from the possibility of a tragic end—both for the governor's son and for his long marriage, about which rumors of divorce were circulating widely at the time.

By best accounts, Michael's raft had capsized, and he and his companion, René Wassing, the translator and art expert assigned by the NNG government to accompany him, had been in the Arafoera Sea for a little more than 24 hours as we were leaving for Hawaii. It would be another 24 hours before we reached New Guinea.

The story of this accident at sea, which ended in the death of a promising young man, includes the improbable saving of his young companion, a fruitless search by sea and air for several days, and a forsaken father's commitment to create a substantial memorial to his youngest son—the Michael C. Rockefeller Wing of the Metropolitan Museum of Art, which would house the fascinating and sometimes beautiful objects that lay at the bottom of his ill-fated adventure.

| November 29, 1961 | **Heider to RG** |

A letter just for you, not the Film Study Center.

It is now ten days. I still cannot come to terms with it. It would be hard to accept the death of anyone in this way. With Michael it is impossible. The next two weeks should give us an answer.

The interviews with you and Eliot were broadcast over Radio Biak last night—it was very fine, Bob, especially your attempt to come to grips with Michael swimming from the raft. It was consistent with the man who went two successive days to the salt wells to get the noise of splashing brine, and the man who found it necessary to bring out the art of the Asmat. If Michael had not been Michael, he would not have tried to swim ashore—and he never would have come to New Guinea. There is only small comfort in this fatalism. But I am very grateful for having known Michael.

| November 30, 1961 | **RG to Gerbrands** |

Mike is lost. We are all terribly saddened, terribly bewildered. I am sorry beyond words that it was not possible for you to stay at Schiphol

Rocky Son Lost in N. Guinea

Boat, 3 Aboard, Drifts to Sea, Governor Flies to Join Hunt

NEW YORK, Monday (UPI)—Gov. Nelson A. Rockefeller's youngest son Michael was reported last night to have disappeared while on a canoe trip collecting primitive art among former headhunting tribes of Dutch New Guinea. Early today his stunned father was off by jet to join an air-sea search. Rockefeller, already beset by personal and political troubles connected with the surprise announcement Friday that his 31-year marriage would end in divorce, was joined on the emergency trip by Michael's twin sister, Mrs. Mary Strawbridge.

The governor also enlisted in his party Dr. Robert G. Gardner, director of the Harvard University film study center, who commanded the scientific expedition that originally took young Rockefeller into the stone-age primitive South Pacific area.

The party left for San Francisco aboard a commercial jet flight, planned to stop overnight in that city and then proceed on to Tokyo where it will charter a plane to New Guinea.

A family spokesman said Mrs. Rockefeller, the former Mary Todhunter Clark of Philadelphia, would remain at home. She and her estranged husband spent the weekend following their divorce announcement on the family estate near suburban Tarrytown, N. Y.

ART-HUNTING TREK

Two of young Rockefeller's Dutch companions also were reported missing on the art-hunting foray along the New Guinea coast into virtually unexplored rain forest and coastal swampland.

The bachelor heir to a vast family fortune has been pretty much on his own since Sept. 4, when the Gardner expedition in which he acted as an audio recorder broke up. It started out last spring to film the life of the Willigiman-Wallalua people, a tribe of warriors. Young Rockefeller had the job of recording such oddities as native teeth-chattering, which a spokesman said he performed "wonderfully."

An account of the mishap from official channels at the Hague, Holland .aid Michael, a 23-year-old scientifically bent Harvard graduate, was boating with two Dutch companions in

Turn to Page 46, Col. 4

TYPICAL NATIVE
More Primitive Than Civilized

MAP locates New Guinea, world's second largest island, where Michael Rockefeller traveled on his expedition.

Hub Family Of 4 Killed In NH Crash

Four members of a Boston family, including two small children, were killed yesterday in a headon crash between two cars on Rte. 101 in Greeland, N. H. State police said the accident was caused by a speeding operator traveling in the wrong lane.

Their deaths hiked the New England highway death toll to 15.

Victims of the tragedy were Mrs. Estelle Goldstein, 29, of 60 Stratton st., Dorchester, her son, Jay, 6 months, daughter, Susan, 8 and her mother Mrs. Pearl Benson 61 of 409 Warren st. Roxbury.

Melvin Goldstein 27 father and husband of the family, was taken to Portsmouth Hospital. Full extent of his injuries were not immediately available.

A third Goldstein child, Lynn, 3, was unharmed.

State police said the vehicle containing the Goldstein's and being operated by Melvin, was rammed by a car operated by Earl H. Coffey, 34, of Walnut ave., North Hampston, N. H. He was also severely injured.

Trooper Lewis Watson said the Goldstein car was in its proper lane on the two-lane highway. He said he spotted the Coffey machine proceeding at a high rate of speed and was preparing to clock the driver's mileage when the accident occurred.

Goldstein was appointed as a motor vehicle inspector only last Tuesday by Registrar Clement A. Riley.

Chief Inspector Max Jacobs said Goldstein was in "the breaking in stage" and hadn't assumed the official duties of an inspector. He was on a day off yesterday.

DESPITE STRAIN, ROCKEFELLER ANSWERS NEWSMEN
Just Before He Boarded Plane on First Leg of Trip
(UPI Telephoto)

Harvard Scientist Aids Rocky in Hunt

A Harvard scientist who led the expedition that took Michael Rockefeller to New Guinea last summer began a long trip back to the huge jungle island last night to help search for him.

Dr. Robert Gardner agreed to go because of his intimate knowledge of the area and after receiving a request from Gov. Nelson Rockefeller, United Press International reported.

Before leaving, Dr. Gardner told the Record American that last summer's expedition was much more perilous than the one on which young Rockefeller is reported lost.

He also disclosed that Michael had remained in New Guinea to study on his own when the Harvard group returned to the U. S. last Sept. 5.

NATIVES FRIENDLY

Dr. Gardner, who heads the university's Film Study Center, said the area in which Michael vanished was wild country but not considered hazardous. He said it is a land of dense jungles, menacing swamps and swift rivers but that the primitive people who dwell there are generally friendly.

Gardner led the expedition on which Michael and other members of the Harvard party penetrated the fierce Midland Mountains of interior New Guinea to film the tribal rites

ROBERT GARDNER
Rocky Asked Him to Help

and warfare of the savages. Besides the ever-present dan-

Turn to Page 47, Col. 1

MRS. NELSON ROCKEFELLER, SON MICHAEL AND THE GOVERNOR
At Harvard in 1960 When They Watched Youngest Son Graduate

Story of Rockefeller's disappearance, *Boston Record American,* November 20, 1961

[Amsterdam's airport] last night. Governor Rockefeller was also very distressed not to see you. He will probably answer your letter, but if he does not I want you to know how much he appreciates your interest and friendship with Michael.

What I want to discuss are plans to publish on the Asmat. Michael's father is anxious to put into a book pictures and writing about the art and culture of this area. I suggested that you might be agreeable to write an article on Asmat art and that you might be willing to share your pictures. Michael's pictures of his trip with you will be available, but much of his material done on his fatal venture is in the Arafoera. I will edit the book and write an introduction. Later I will send you details, but what I would like now is your consent or refusal to write the article, plus coming to New York to help identify Michael's collection, plus giving some lectures in New York and/or other cities about the art of the Asmat.

November 30, 1961 **RG to Broekhuyse, in Biak, New Guinea**

The trip from Merauke [the principal town on the Asmat coast] was long and exhausting. Every stop (Manila, Bangkok, Calcutta, Karachi, Cairo, Rome, Frankfort, Amsterdam, New York City) had its local press, getting the latest on Mike's tragedy. Amsterdam was a real crush, of course. I had no chance to try to find Gerbrands, lost somewhere in the mob, who had come up from Leiden to see Governor Rockefeller.

I believe that the press has for the most part *not* confused the Baliem expedition with Mike's Asmat venture.

KLM forgot Mike's bag with the cameras in Amsterdam—they will follow in a matter of days. As soon as they are repaired (God knows how long from now) I will send them to you, hopefully before the New Year. Many thanks for your help and interest and loyalty.

In this period, Heider was in quite frequent letter-writing contact, filling me in with news of what we all had left behind and what he was required by his circumstances to see. I was often disturbed by what I read, especially about the individuals to whom I had inevitably become deeply attached. One of them was Pua, the little swineherd who would be my principal young player in the film, and the other was Weyak, who would be the mature male leading player and exemplar of Dani manhood.

December 4, 1961 **Heider to RG**

The tragedy of Michael Rockefeller has taken a long time to sink in—partly because of the scanty news and the uncertainty, partly because I have been here, where he was so very much alive, where the people still ask me when he is coming back.

Weyak was severely mauled (clubs) a few days ago over garden rights. I have been treating a 15-cm scalp wound—very nasty. But the internal injuries seem to be the worst—he called Jegé Asuk over from the police post (!) to bleed him this morning. All this is a sign of jumpiness caused by the ending of battles, and by their insecurity about the intentions of the police. I expect a good deal more of it in the next months.

December 18, 1961

Broekhuyse to RG

Many thanks for your letter. Since you left here I had not had the slightest information about Mike. The rescue effort was continuing, and up to now I had not heard anything about results. I had *no* expenses as far as my going to Merauke is concerned. How dreadful the circumstances were, though I was happy to see you and Eliot again. Some strange bond grew between us all in the expedition. Michael's death made it even stranger.

January 3, 1962

RG to de Bruyn

So much has transpired lately I hardly know where to start. I will see Governor and Mrs. Rockefeller again next week, but, for now, I can report that they both have accustomed themselves to the reality of Michael's death.

I hear often from Karl, who has shown no sign of panic regarding his situation in the dispute over Netherlands New Guinea. I'm sure you will keep him informed as far as emergencies are concerned. Otherwise he seems to be doing a remarkably rewarding and productive piece of work.

By early 1962 I had made some inroads editing the approximately twenty hours of New Guinea screen time available to fashion a film. This was a modest figure for a nonfiction film in those days. Far greater amounts of film became commonplace as cinéma vérité took hold. In my circumstances I found it useful to make provisional continuities that highlighted what I was thinking would be important in a final result. These provisional lists of shots, or outlines, evolved as ideas changed in the process of coming to know the material better through its frequent screening. It is a rudiment of film editing that when shots or sequences are viewed in different contexts, preceding or following new and different shots and sequences, their visual effect and so also their meaning are also being refined. By early January 1962 I was seeing the benefit of a return to Homoak to look for answers to some questions about meaning and fact, questions that had arisen from my editing.

January 10, 1962

RG to Heider

I hope to get there in June. Right now the biggest obstacle looks to be the Indonesians. The smell of war gets stronger and stronger. If that doesn't come off, I expect the Dutch will simply give in.

I want to suggest strongly that you send your notes here frequently. Also, please consider the advisability of shipping what material culture you have collected to date *now*. If the Indonesians come, there will be too much confusion and no transport.

Dirt about the expedition was printed in Europe and Australia. Boendermaker [a high-ranking NNG official] said, when on leave in Holland during Mike's tragedy, that he was a rash young man, paying too much for skulls, etc., etc. Also, he mentioned that the Baliem expedition had had a brush with the missionaries and government. So far not one Dutch official has come out unequivocally to deny the rumors. The Australian press has stooped to outrageous rumors about shrunken heads, raids for heads, and paid warfare. However, don't worry about this at all—everyone here is completely behind us and understands the situation very well. Frankly, I am not the least bothered and don't expect to be in the future.

January 11, 1962   **RG to Broekhuyse**

I am sending a series of short articles I did for the *Boston Globe*. They were done terribly quickly when the publisher asked me as a favor to do something during the crisis period. I thought you might be amused at what an "anti-Dutch" American feels. It is too bad that some of your countrymen feel they have to explain things by giving me such a name. Perhaps my greatest regret about everything that has happened is that no man in a high post in New Guinea has seen fit to deny the absurd rumors about the expedition—not even Plateel [governor of Netherlands New Guinea], who refused to do so when I asked him to in Merauke. He said instead that "what we did was all right but very difficult to defend." Despite this attitude, I don't find it difficult to defend the Dutch in New Guinea, because I feel very strongly that their intentions are more honorable than the Indonesians'.

January 11, 1962   **Heider to RG**

I listen to the news about us daily. I am making no plans for leaving, and won't unless they throw me out. By the way, the enthusiasm for Papua Barat is great and, I think, mostly genuine. They have a flag, a song, and a name, and now a growing sense of identification. If Sukarno does take the country, he will be stuck with an area which is not only economically useless, but politically resentful.

January 27, 1962   **Heider to RG**

Your plans for coming back are excellent. You will be most welcome. The *akuni* [local people] still ask about you almost daily.

The situation here gets worse.

January 29, 1962   **RG to Heider**

Is there any chance of you recording 10–30 seconds of the *yoroik* [mourning dove] singing? It is most necessary for the total feel and development of the film.

111

✓ – ok
o – more to do

"DEAD BIRDS"

June 1-62

(tentative continuity)

1. Lizard   o   *BIRD – Get Bird in Fields –*

2. Frontier-from Tukumba o

3. Weaklekek in Honai-Seq. he eats breakfast o

4. Warabara from honai (established in #2) ✓

5. Homaklep from hill behind Sili-early AM no activity outside ✓
5A. *weaklekek starts a njeakané in honai* o
6. Lizard o

7. Lizard and Wuperainma o

8. Tukom eatin his breakfast in Lise ✓

      ******Lyric introduction of Tukom******* *OR IMAM BIRD CU –*
           frogs jumping in ditches   o
           Bannana tree flapping in breeze ✱ ✓
           storm coming across valley   ✱ ✓
           empty honai   o

9. Weaklekek starts for gaio (over Anelerak) Sequence ✓

10. Tukom starts for ~~Alima~~ *Abukulmo* with pigs-Sequence ✱ o

11. women leave Homaklep to work in gardens   o

12. Tukom in Alima pig gardens   ✓ *(Tukom looks at Abukulmo – cut to Eak)*
12A – EAK comes out of Honai into sun — sequence –
13. Hanomoak walking to gardens   ✓

14. Weaklekek climbs gaio   o ✓

15. women wait on Anelerak   o o

16. Weaklekek comes down from gaio goes into garden o

17. women proceed o

18. Hanomoak and Jege Asuk begin to work ✓ ✱ ?

19. Uwar hunting bird above Wuperainma AM in Yugulilu ✓

20.   *********Lric Introduction of Uwar*********
           kainman killing; huge pig   ✓
           hawk whistles down Tukumba   ✓
           warrior on Warabara-slow motion   o
           Aikhe very full bears down on ducks, they scatter o

21. Uwar hunting joined by Aplegma (Ap. first seen in #3) ?

22. U and A throw spears and then race down toward Homaklep ?

23. Weaklekek working with women in garden ✓

24. Tukom joined by friends in ~~Alima~~ *Abukulmo –* ✓

An early continuity for *Dead Birds*

I doubt now that I can get the long film *[Dead Birds]* finished by June, with all the work entailed and all the extra things I've been doing. I have to get some assistance somehow soon, but even so there is probably too much to do. If this is the case, I would come out with the edited work-print just to show the government, and finish the sound, etc., next fall.

As the spring of 1962 made its appearance, I had been actively editing for about four months and it was clear that I had a long way to go, especially if I wanted something to show to even a restricted audience. From time to time I still did outlines or what might be called continuities, in which I jotted down the story line or progression of events toward some sort of conclusion or denouement. The narrative sequence was frequently on my mind and sometimes written down—reminders or models, to be improved upon later, or even renounced.

In 1972, Karl Heider asked me to write an essay, "On the Making of Dead Birds,*" for a publication he was getting out called* An Ethnographic Companion to the Film Dead Birds. *The year 1972 is not at too great a remove from late 1964, when I felt my film was finished, so I will quote here from what I wrote for the* Ethnographic Companion:

> I edited *Dead Birds* in the basement of the Peabody Museum at Harvard. I had not heard of a Steenbeck or any other of the now indispensable editing tables in common use by editors. Nor did I have much use for a Moviola since the shooting I had done was not with a [sound] synchronized camera. I used four and sometimes five Bell & Howell [16mm] viewers on as many tables arranged so that I could shift quickly from one image or sequence to another. I also had a projector, and the film, as it went together, would be constantly taken off the rewinds and screened. This was indispensable because the viewers were so small and also because once the scale was increased to at least life size, and preferably beyond that, it was possible to see, really for the first time, what the image contained.

I have forgotten exactly when John Marshall came back from New Haven and his studies in anthropology at Yale, but Tim Asch was working in the Peabody Museum basement at the time I was editing Dead Birds *and his hands were full of projects he and John were embarking on together. When I was not physically editing* Dead Birds, *I was holding a workshop in filmmaking an evening or two each week, doing the modest administration called for by an underfinanced and understaffed Film Study Center, and planning the interior spaces of the Carpenter Center for the Visual Arts, then in its initial construction phase. Construction was completed in 1963, at which time the Film Study Center and my editing facilities were moved into it.*

Owing to a prevailing principle of academic freedom, I was free to choose the way I would work on Dead Birds. *No deadlines were imposed except my own, and neither J. O. Brew nor any other authority at Harvard would have dreamed of saying I was taking too much time, much less that I should or shouldn't be making this or that kind of film.*

In the Companion article mentioned above, I also wrote the following, which attests to an important concern whenever a film is under construction—its title:

A warrior dressed for battle

Finally, a word about the choice of *Dead Birds* as a title. I knew before I left New Guinea that I would use it. In fact, this title and especially the implications that it contained for me had a significant effect on what I saw and therefore what I filmed. In the opening sequence of the film I try to explain that the Dani identify themselves with birds. This does not happen to the exclusion of all other devices or symbols, but it is a dominant motif in both their mythic and mundane lives. *Dead Birds* is a translation from the Dani term for weapons, ornaments, and other articles captured in warfare. They represent, magically, victims on the other side. In fact they sometimes are referred to not as *sué warek* (dead birds) but *ap warek* (dead men). It is appropriate also to remember that Dani men take ardent advantage of the extraordinary variety of birds that dwell in or near their Valley. A Dani is a plumed warrior in his most desirous state. What I have done is to acknowledge this indubitable fact and be glad for its wry, perhaps ironic, implications. I saw the Dani people, feathered and fluttering men and women, as enjoying the fate of all men and women. They dressed their lives with plumage, but faced as certain death as the rest of us drabber souls. The film attempts to say something about how we all, as humans, meet our animal fate.

Having this title with all it contained was vital for me while editing. During the months of spring still to come, I made as much progress as possible with a mind filled with such thoughts.

February 13, 1962

RG to Heider

Another two weeks have flashed by and I seem to be about where I have been since getting back. Objectively we have accomplished a great deal, I'm glad to say. All the photographs are printed and in albums and almost completely annotated. The film is on its way through the cutting stage. Articles and books are getting shaped up.

February 26, 1962

RG to Heider

The missionary gossip starts again. You should read the Binghampton [newspaper] account first. Obviously Lake [a Baliem Valley missionary] likes publicity and obviously the press is eager for a story on Nelson Rockefeller, even if it is only through his only very lately lamented son. I regret enormously that the Dutch have not stepped more vigorously on the dangerous nonsense promulgated. All I can

Cremation of a warrior

Rocky's Son Stirred New Guinea Wars--Missionary

Sought Films Of Fighting, Says Cleric

By MARILYN J. YOUNG

A Binghamton - born missionary who met Michael Rockefeller in New Guinea said young Rockefeller and other members of the Harvard expedition stirrred up wars among the natives

Members of the Harvard group, explained the Rev. H. M. Lake, wanted to take movies of every phase possible of tribal life.

Mr. Rockefeller

REMINDERS OF HOME—The Rev. and Mrs. H. M. Lake and t h e i r children, Larry, 10, and Karen, 8, inspect several souvenirs from the Baliem Valley of Dutch New Guinea where they will return to missionary d u t i e s in July.

Article in the *Binghamton* (NY) *News*, 1962

say at this point is that everyone seems pretty well satisfied that the story is what I, not the missionaries, say it is.

We are moving ahead on all fronts.

March 13, 1962

Heider to RG

I dread looking at the calendar these days. Soon it will be one year since Michael and I came from the opposite sides of the earth to meet in Biak, and then to go on to all the rest. I wonder what the *akuni* think of him. They know he drowned in the Asmat. They mention him—and the rest of you—someone manages to bring it up every day. I don't know what they think of anything.

March 29, 1962

RG to Heider

I will still try to get out in June or July, despite what looks like difficulties over visas.

I've seen publishers in New York City about the Baliem picture book *[Gardens of War],* and there is no problem getting it done. The question is with whom and how. I'm tremendously pleased that there was as much in the stills as there turns out to be. There is good material on a couple of funerals, very good boys' games, and excellent portraits. It will be an enormous job selecting the best.

I have just read Peter's final draft and I think it a fine piece of work. Nothing about the expedition—no sense of precise time, and full of good information. My only criticism is that he might lean more toward understatement.

RG to Broekhuyse

My plans remain the same—to come to New Guinea around the middle of June. I suppose now that there will be trouble getting a visa for your territory since the threat of invasion is growing. I will try.

All response so far to the photographs I have shown has been excited. The Asmat book will be pictures plus text, like the Baliem book.

The film is coming. I will have only a provisional cut (pre-montage) when and if I get to New Guinea in June. But it will show the basic outline of the story.

Peter's book will be published in November. There is no question in my mind that his book will not interfere in any way with publishing you might want to do. Both Karl and I hope that you will write up your material. If it becomes possible for you to come here, perhaps you can have the freedom and the illustrational material to write some fine articles.

April 23, 1962

RG to Heider

Just spent the whole weekend with Peter. Very worthwhile for us both. We worked out the problem of photographs for books (both of us are satisfied), and we worked over the first cut of *Dead Birds*. From our viewing I can see there is a film—perhaps a very long film, as long as three hours. There is about a month for me to work on it until Lee leaves by boat for Europe with the children. Then I will go over it again with Peter for final touch-up before—hopefully—leaving for New Guinea in mid June.

April 26, 1962

RG to Netherlands Consul General Slingenberg, New York

When Mr. Michael Rockefeller was lost off the Asmat coast, after the expedition had ended, I returned with Governor Rockefeller. During that very melancholy stay, I had the opportunity to talk with Governor Plateel about the expedition's plans for further work. The plan of such work was to keep one member, Karl Heider, in the Baliem doing sustained fieldwork and for me to return for a brief visit. It is my hope to spend from three to five weeks with Mr. Heider in the months of June and July. Besides filling in answers to questions concerning the Grand Valley people that have come up since I returned, I want to show, in Hollandia, the film which was made during our stay last year.

May 7, 1962

RG to Heider

I hope to reach Hollandia June 17th. I will send you a cable when everything is certain. I'm excited about it, though I don't like having to do so much in such a short time.

Yesterday there was a memorial service in Tarrytown for Michael. Just family and friends. Vic de Bruyn was there, and he will come here next Sunday. The service was short, unemotional, and very Baptist. Some prayers, some hymns, and a moving tribute by a Scottish minister. It is the finally recognized termination of Michael, and all the family was very composed.

May 12, 1962

Heider to RG

This has been a very sad time for the *akuni*. The flu, which killed some 60 people to the south a month ago, slowly made its way downstream, and has been here for the last two weeks. Most of us here got it. Yesterday a woman died and was burned. This was the first person I really knew and felt close to, who died. Wali was moved—I have never seen anyone so moved. In the last months, he has been very close to her. Their relationship was as near our ideas of love as anything I have been able to see here. He stayed inside most of the day, mourning loudly, recognizing no one. Siba, her brother, was almost as moved, but he was silent, taking an active part in all the work. The pyre was laid, the atmosphere grew tense, and the men argued about the last logs. Then she was brought out, her face covered with a net, and was laid on the flames. Suddenly Wali ran forward, jumped onto the pyre, and tried to throw himself onto her body, saying he too wanted to burn. He was pulled back. For a few moments, he stood crying and holding out his hands towards the flames. You may find pictures of it—I'm afraid the camera was not being held very steadily.

May 17, 1962

RG to Broekhuyse

I have received the visa, so unless something peculiar happens I will arrive in Biak the 18th of June. Perhaps you could arrange for a projector to look at the film.

May 26, 1962

Broekhuyse to RG

Do you have any objection to showing your film in an open-air theater, so that many more people can look at it (civil authorities and marine officers—we can exclude journalists, etc.)? If you do not agree, I will try to arrange a projector to show the film in my home.

May 31, 1962

RG to Matthiessen

Just to be a little more specific about the *Dead Birds* conversation we had this morning, let me say that if something dire befalls me between now and September, I would hope that you could supervise the final execution of the film. You appreciate, better than anyone else, the points made by the sequences I have cut. Essentially, the suspense I want to create in order to hold the audience hangs on the question, who is going to get killed next—specifically, I try to suggest

118

that it will be a boy; that it will happen near the Aikhé, which is Weyak's responsibility, etc. In more general terms I am trying to portray a mood of watchfulness and aggressiveness which is based on different aims than our own, but also convey, despite this, that the blood involved is a high price to pay (even when it gives the men such pleasure and the society its coherence).

The sounds should be drawn *entirely* from the recorded tapes of dance, work, conversation, pig sticking, birds, etc., etc. I cannot say what sound goes exactly where, because I haven't yet thought it through. But I know that I want to avoid any "incidental" or "background" sounds. No *picon* [mouth harp] where there is no *picon* visible. Perhaps one exception would be a particularly hideous pig squeal in the sequence where Weaké is "killed" (the *kaio* shots). It is a film about revenge among people who are capable of deep feelings of remorse and elation. You know it, and with Karl's help and a very good editor there is no problem to finish.

My letter to Peter was both a request that he supervise the completion of **Dead Birds** *should anything prevent me from doing it myself and an opportunity to relate to him, in a somewhat oblique manner, the nature of a few of the central threads and devices I had used in the film's construction. It is consistent with the incomplete but meaningful sketches I composed from time to time as I crafted the film.*

June 2, 1962

RG to Broekhuyse

I want only you to see the film. One exception could be the resident at Biak. He was the man I talked with at the KLM Hotel during the Governor's trip. The reason I don't want people is that the film is not finished. It is only a silent, visual continuity.

The reason I returned to New Guinea to visit Karl in the araucaria forest where I had lived—and about which I still dreamed—was to elicit his reactions and listen to his suggestions, particularly on points of fact. The film I had put together reflected my thinking and interpretation of a culture I knew less well, at least in detail, than he. I was also still engrossed in solving the dilemma I saw gathering strength concerning my intentions as a filmmaker and my scruples as an anthropologist.

I had certain hesitancies concerning the role of fiction in the depiction of behavior. How much of a fabulist could I be without damaging my credibility as a witness? As I worked, I found many answers to these kinds of questions, including the proposition that anthropology was itself engaged in making things up. What is the "ethnographic present," in which almost all monographs I had ever read couched their findings, but a fiction? I suffered also the misgiving, provided us all by even the faintest immersion in surreality, of thinking that anything that is not absurd and, I would add, ambiguous is probably not real. It could be said that my outlook, to the extent that it was influenced by my training as an anthropologist, was not likely always to be in harmony with my outlook as an artist.

My trip was relatively short. I showed the work-print I brought with me to a small group in Hollandia that included Broekhuyse, de Bruyn, and a few others. I recall there being little conversation following the screening— partly, I suppose, for the reason that the film was clearly an account that gave major emphasis to the sensitive issue of tribal warfare, ritual or otherwise, and also because these kinds of showings cannot be seen by most people as being anything but sadly unfinished, even crude. There was no sound. I imagine it was something of a disappointment.

My time in the midst of Dani friends, however, was quite overwhelming in the fondness they expressed and the generosity of spirit they showed. While there I did little work of a visual nature other than still photography, which upon my return to Cambridge was inadvertently thrown in the trash by an overzealous janitor.

July 18, 1962

Heider to RG

The very welcome ripples you caused in my vast sea of Dani months have disappeared, and only when I throw out an empty wine bottle do I remember that your visit was real.

Here are some notes on *Dead Birds,* about things I can remember. It seems to me I mentioned a lot more to you when you were here. On the whole I was terribly impressed with the film—overwhelmed would be a better word—and am very proud to have contributed even my few pedestrian feet.

September 27, 1962

RG to Broekhuyse

You will see the fruits of all our labors on behalf of *Life Magazine.* Fortunately they allowed me to write the piece, even though their *editors present* it. You took one of the pictures, the battle scene across two pages. Karl, Sam, and Michael took the others. Eliot took one, the shot of two women dancing. I hope you approve. I feel it is the best job *Life* has done for a long time.

I haven't the least notion what is happening in New Guinea. There is no news anymore. I'm glad you are staying.

October 9, 1962

Heider, in Vienna, to RG

I shall take October off as vacation and aim for Cambridge November 1st. Our *Life* article is on the streets. Very exciting to see something so concrete. Your contribution—the text—is the best feature.

November 7, 1962

Matthiessen to RG

I enclose a review [of *Under the Mountain Wall*] from the *Washington Post* which is no less infuriating for being generally favorable: in an attempt to assert his own tenuous expertise, the reviewer calls into question not only my own integrity but—since I state that you and Karl and Broekhuyse checked it over for errors and distortions, and that the events are real, etc.—that of the expedition itself, referring twice to the book as a work of fiction. The reviewer's inability to distinguish between fiction and a creative treatment of fact is not the point: after six books, I am hardened to such. But his smug conviction that I have not been honest about the missionaries, etc., that my approach is spurious, is intolerable. The reception to date is a little disheartening; my approach seems to make people suspicious, since they do not know how to pigeonhole the book—what the hell is it? Well, I tell myself that all original approaches to *anything* are treated with suspicion, and I'm still convinced this approach was the best one. I really don't regret it. And it must be said that about one reviewer out of four gets the scent of what I'm after and goes into a raving fit; perhaps these will infect the rest.

Peter's book was a familiar matter by the time we had left to return to our respective lives in the western world. The typewriter Peter used daily—and frequently nightly—in New Guinea was never far from the bedroll I occupied next to his. What always impressed me was the diligence Peter applied to his writing. It seemed he was intent on having his account finished on the day he departed, almost as if what he was doing was reportage. In some ways I think it was, especially in the extraordinary attention he gave to detail. Of course, it was clear to me before we ever set out that his coming would mean having a companion whose interests were novelistic as well as naturalistic. I had read Peter's early novels, along with his work on North American birds, and thought that I saw a sensibility attuned to the phenomenal world sympathetic to my own. Sympathetic, perhaps, but by no means parallel. Our scruples were similar but not identical.

April 3, 1963

RG to Heider, in New Guinea

Joyce Chopra [a rising filmmaker in Cambridge] is helping me now. *Dead Birds* gets done—I hope for an answer-print in May. I look forward to getting your news and film.

There is an aptness to the term "answer-print," in that when it is viewed it contains answers to an immensity of questions that begin to arise early in the filmmaking process. The innumerable doubts, suspicions, fears, and even hopes that a filmmaker entertains while shooting and editing find clarification in an answer-print. An answer-print is a sort of proof made from the original film stock, in this case a fine-grained reversal material called Ektachrome. The images produced are of the highest possible quality. Subsequent prints will almost invariably be second- and even third- or fourth-generation copies, which are degraded in terms of acuity, contrast, and other measures of fidelity to the original cinematography.

An answer-print also gives the filmmaker answers concerning the soundtrack, which until the print is made has not been properly heard. In the weeks leading up to making the first answer-print (another would be made after shortening the film), I required help editing the sound and assisting in a number of the routines surrounding post-production, as the editing of a film is often called. For these purposes I was helped by a sound technician, Jairus Lincoln, and by the editor Joyce Chopra.

The last task before an answer-print is produced is called "conforming," in which the original film is assembled in conformity with a work-print, a finalized and low-fidelity, often black-and-white, model of the completed film.

May 2, 1963

RG to Broekhuyse, in the Netherlands

I have been so busy working on *Dead Birds* that there has been no time to write. It is wonderful to hear that your thesis has been started and that you will have the time to pursue it seriously and steadily. The work on the photo book *[Gardens of War]* has been impeded by all the other things.

May 3, 1963

Heider to RG

Local news: the *mawé* [major ceremony of weddings] seems definitely under way—at least the first steps. Kurelu has declared all pigs *wusa* [affected by black magic], and the *akuni* are planting large new gardens and beginning to talk about it. The ceremonies themselves are still several months away.

May 6, 1963

RG to Heider

We are cutting the camera original of *Dead Birds* now. I hope to be in California May 28th to make a print for showing at the Loeb Drama Center at Harvard. We are all working very hard, and it will be done soon.

June 24, 1963

RG to Heider

Quite a lot is happening on *Dead Birds*. It has had what seems to be a unanimously good acceptance, from Robert Lowell to Joseph *(The Sky Above, The Mud Below)* Levine. Levine may want it for theatrical release, which will keep me pretty busy.

Despite my independence with respect to the usual constraints of tight budgets, deadlines, and even issues of content, there are always anxieties concerning the outcome of an ambitious film venture. Would it be successful, and if it is, in what ways? Who would undertake its marketing or distribution? I had to get answers to these questions, which accounts for the involvement of Hollywood producer Joseph E. Levine. I also had to think of a way for the work to be premiered, which often determines a film's future. A person in my position can sometimes be shameless enough to ask, as I did of Heider, if there was a way to film the amputation (iki palin) of a young girl's finger jointsfor possible inclusion in a less-than-likely wide-scale theatrical release by Levine.

July 9, 1963

RG to Heider

I'm still negotiating the distribution of *Dead Birds*. I should hear this week from Levine. Can you get me an *iki palin* sequence? Preferably authentic, but use your theatrical and filmic imagination to get me an editable sequence. We should have this documented anyway, but it may possibly come in quite handy if I were to make a commercial version of *Dead Birds*. The real film is made and will survive. But the theatrical is not and anyway it wouldn't survive, but we could all make a lot more films if it gets done.

I leave in about two weeks for Europe, to show *Dead Birds* to the Dutch Information Service, review Parisian contacts, and work out European distribution, if Levine fails to come through.

August 13, 1963

RG to Heider

If you haven't done the *iki palin,* don't, because Levine and I have not come to terms and it looks as though we never will. The deal hinged on a total remake of the film—everything seen in one flashback from the war footage, with inserts of Michael Rockefeller salting the whole roast. The past few weeks have not turned up much except some excited screeners. I did show it to the Netherlands Information people and to various personages in Paris. There is a good chance that Europe will see it in theaters, but it will take years in the U.S. There is always T.V., and the slow but steady 16mm business.

While in Paris I arranged for a *Paris Match* story. They will use the *Life* text and slant it pictorially more than scientifically.

August 15, 1963

Heider to RG

My ethnographic work comes along. I still grapple with the bird theme. Each sib has a bird, a special type, which they call *ninakalak* or "classificatory brother." In the beginning, when everything was together, the birds were people. Nakmarugi, the culture hero, then told the birds that they were birds, and they took off to fly around and make noises like proper birds. But they still have this relation to the people. I think you are right with your man-bird symbolism—but I am trying to dig out more specifics. Also, the *etai-eken* [seeds of singing] has a double meaning: the anatomical heart, which even birds and pigs have; and the personality essence, which only comes into normal size when a kid begins to talk with understanding and fluency.

In the late summer of 1963, I had arranged with Peter to bring the first answer-print of Dead Birds *to show to an audience of friends at William Styron's house in Roxbury, Connecticut. Peter was comfortable with those invited because they were literary people whom he liked and respected, Robert Penn Warren and Terry Southern among them. I was agreeable because I knew that Mike Nichols and Lillian Hellman would come, too. They were from a world not that distant from where I was situated except that both were deeply committed to the stage and screen in their commercial guises.*

This occasion was arranged to provide friends with unexpected views of a world they could not have imagined and to extract from them helpful criticism with respect to the film's chances of holding and even engaging an audience. I recall many expressions of wonder on the part of the assembled group, despite the inevitable distractions of highball replenishing, tripping over the projector's electrical connection, late summer light leaking through inadequate curtaining of the screen, and so on.

Late summer, 1963

Matthiessen to RG

Here are suggested cuts in the narration, showing very roughly the kind of thing I thought superfluous, or rather, contributing less to clarity than it took away from mood, from the sense of awe which this film must inspire if it is to succeed on its best level.

I talked with Bill [Styron] again on Monday. He agrees with Lillian [Hellman] that 10–15 minutes should be cut. And shortening is a solution of sorts, I suppose, though I still don't think it is the best one: material as strong as this needs less cutting than pacing. A leaner narration would help: the film cannot hope to instruct its audience in 90 minutes, but it can hope to *illuminate* it—even if the narration contributed as much in information as it takes away in mood, you must ask yourself if you are gaining by the exchange. Bold camera strokes, bold juxtapositions, bold use of recorded sound convey far better what is truly original in this film, the "morning of time" sense of newness, freshness, mystery—in New Guinea, I recall my extreme exasperation at trying to catch in words, words, words that kind of ineffable simplicity that was so patently pictorial. Do you remember how we felt in those first weeks, when we first *saw*? It would have been plenty exciting even if we hadn't had the faintest inkling of what the hell was going on. If this film can make the audience feel one twentieth of our excitement, our *astonishment,* it will be a classic.

I realize it's very easy to speak loosely of what might entail a lot of work for someone else, and it may be that the point is past when any important changes can be made; there is always such a point, in every work, and many things have been ruined when it wasn't recognized. Lillian and I felt badly that we should carp and pick at it in the very face of all that praise you were getting at Styron's, and especially when the praise was well deserved; you might consider, however, that we did so not only because we are closer to the film and know better what, good as it is, it could be, but because, more familiar with what went into its making (for example, recalling that camera brace, my admiration for the visual clarity is boundless), our admiration is actually greater and more real, as well as our concern that you make the most of such material, acquired with such great effort. I'm putting all this badly, but you get the picture.

More correspondence with Peter and conversations with others who were at the Styron screening led me to consider shortening the initial cut of Dead Birds *by about 20 minutes. I felt at the time, and do now, that I could perfectly well have lengthened the film by more than the number of minutes I was thinking of shortening it. When I came to make the final and shorter version, I wanted to try and put into words what I took the central meaning of the film to be. My final utterance in the narration of the film goes as follows:*

> Soon both men and birds will surrender to the night. They will rest for the life and death of days to come. For each, both wait, but with the difference that men, having foreknowledge of their doom, bring a special passion to their life. They will not simply wait for death, nor will they bear it lightly when it comes. Instead, they will try with measured violence to fashion fate themselves. They kill to save their souls and, perhaps, to ease the burden of knowing what birds will never know and what they as men, who have forever killed each other, cannot forget.

I have felt for as long as I have thought about this film and the whole experience of finding and making it that it contained something akin to an epic quality. I had no illusions that any final cut I made would be epic, only that what we had all witnessed and in our various ways expressed, transpired in something close to heroic space and time.

February 21, 1964

Matthiessen to RG

Was very pleased to see the final version of *Dead Birds* the other night—and impressed all over again by your achievement. This version wiped away my qualifications of last time except the one which must be shared by all the expedition members: I wish it was 300 minutes.

In the arena of filmmaking, assumptions about coming to an end have no relation to the facts. Film is unlike its sister arts. When, for example, a painting is done, it is usually left alone, as is also an object carved in wood

Harvard film wins annual Flaherty prize

A color documentary produced by the Film Studies Center of Harvard University has won the 1963 Robert J. Flaherty Award. Competition for the annual prize is sponsored by the Institute of Film Techniques at the City College of New York.

Robert Gardner directed the winning 83-minute film, titled "Dead Birds." The sound was recorded under the supervision of the late Michael Rockefeller.

The film deals with the lives of Papuan natives in the mountains of New Guinea. Margaret Mead, noted anthropologist, said the prize-winning film: "In its making, art neither has been subordinated to, nor has it been allowed to overrule science."

The Flaherty award was presented May 13 in ceremonies in New York.

Announcement of the Flaherty Award in *Variety*, May 12, 1964

or stone. Poets are known to have a continuing authorial connection to their verses, and prose writers sometimes revise their productions. But film for decades exacts larger demands from its makers through its constant need not so much of revision as of promotion, marketing, physical care, and other such attentions. So it is that this tale of **Dead Birds** is not over yet and may not be until time and neglect have taken their ultimate toll.

With the answer-print in hand, I was able to arrange viewings for those who seemed to matter most: my New Guinea team members, co-workers in Cambridge, some distributors, and interested friends and family. The film had still to be more or less officially premiered or debuted. As it happened, Nathan Pusey, then President of Harvard, asked to see it. When he had, he made the decision to show it to an invited audience. This was in October 1963, and I remember being required to dress in a tuxedo: the artist-in-black-turtleneck era had not yet arrived. So it was at least a debut, and a more conventional premiere could still take place.

Despite mild carping by a few faculty members who could not see why one of their youngest colleagues was given such a grand forum for his labors at the university, the film's reception was all I could possibly have wanted. The major dissatisfaction was my own. I would say to whoever would listen that the film had still to be shortened and that I should take immediate heed of its critique at the hands of Matthiessen, Hellman, and a few others. For the next several months, this is what I worked on, quite certain that shortening was needed but unsure at times how to do it. In the end, I removed around 20 minutes of treasured scenes, but ones I was content to believe were slowing the narrative even as they continued to remind me of my initial astonishments.

Sometimes I have thought of going back to the elements from which Dead Birds was composed and giving a whole new shape to them. But this would be unduly arduous, and it would take too long. Maybe I could just rewrite the narration, which I have often thought too heavy and occasionally arch. Perhaps I will do this someday, now that computers have made editing so much easier. These kinds of thoughts are related to the point

CONCLUSO A FIRENZE IL QUINTO FESTIVAL DEI POPOLI

Il «Marzocco d'oro» assegnato ad un film americano

Florence Film Festival grand prize notice, *Giornale dello Spettacolo,* February 1, 1964

I made earlier about film requiring endless maintenance. I have not even mentioned the need for keeping its constituent parts near freezing and dust free, if it is expected to endure the ages in the way that other products of the arts can be made to do.

Once the official 83-minute version of Dead Birds *was made, the film began to make the festival rounds, getting what seemed like excellent reception and winning numerous prizes, including a quite large number of Italian lira as Grand Prize winner at the Florence Film Festival in 1964. I converted the lira into a ruined house near the cathedral on the acropolis of Ibiza, where I had been urged to go the previous summer. In the early sixties, Ibiza was as unknown as the Baliem Valley, and the resident women, all dressed in black, threw stones at their European counterparts in trousers. Of course, all of that didn't last long, and my Balearic retreats came quickly to an end.*

For a year I worked more as an agent, publicist, and general promoter than as the filmmaker of a product that had succeeded in generating uncommon attention from both the media world and the academic community. The still memorable events surrounding the death of Michael Rockefeller seemed to give the public an awareness of the planet's second largest island it had never had before. Still, beyond its geographical and biographical interest, Dead Birds *appeared to grip many viewers by means of the undeniable and proximate actuality of its depiction of human violence, a violence that was caught at a pivotal moment in the long chronicle of human history, when a society situated in the neolithic was about to become modernized.*

But could I say with any confidence that my early and naïve hope had in some way succeeded, that witnessing on film people waging ritual war might shed light on other wars and other rituals? I am not at all sure. In any case, by the end of 1964 Dead Birds *had become more a left- than right-brain matter for me, and I had already set out to find the next film.*

Gardner films Weyak, Kurelu, Pua, and Wali watching *Dead Birds*, January 1989

coda

Between 1964 when Dead Birds *was released and the present day, time has wrought its inevitable consequences, what Susan Sontag called its "melt," on those who participated in the making of that film. I witnessed some of this on a visit in 1996 to our araucaria forest home, by then mostly cut down to provide lumber for a police post. I was told the little swineherd, Pua, had died of cancer and that Weyak, my leading man, had given up his ghost as well. Of course, the natural landscape too had been altered by the ravages of mindless modernity. This was powerfully evident in a largely impassable road that cuts a meandering scar the length of the Baliem River valley floor. In Wamena a few small hostels have been built by Javanese immigrants for infrequent tourists who are under permanent attack from Dani souvenir merchants hawking inauthentic tribal wares. By natural cunning and chance, Wali lives on, as do several others in our original, 1961, band of filmmaking co-conspirators.*

Many of the Dani I had known years ago have since that time seen themselves in photocopies of photographs in Gardens of War, *shown to them by intrepid foreigners, and on a day during a visit of mine in late 1988 to early 1989, a select group that included Kurelu, Weyak, Pua, and Wali saw themselves in* Dead Birds, *when I ran the film for their entertainment using a small video monitor.*

Everyone heard what befell Michael Rockefeller almost as soon as it happened. They probably have not yet heard that Michael's friend Sam Putnam died in 2006 from a rare neurological disorder, or even that Eliot Elisofon died suddenly of a heart attack in 1973. But they do know that Jan Broekhuyse, Karl Heider, Peter Matthiessen, and I are enjoying active lives.

As for the chronicle of the film itself, it has continued to evolve for the almost forty-three years since its debut screening in October 1964. Television has shown the film in dozens of countries, and with the advent of such media as DVD it can be seen virtually anywhere at any time. Even its historic preservation may be secured by its having been put on the National Register of American Films in the Library of Congress.

But despite the fact that this film has been a staple visual experience for at least two generations in my own society (was this in order to open western eyes to almost unimaginable "otherness?"), I have seen little evidence of the slightest diminishment in human bellicosity and obsession with violence. Nor does it seem likely that the word "ritual" as a modifier alters much the meaning of the word "war." Nevertheless, the opening of eyes to "otherness" as a way of showing evidence of "oneness" is a hope I continue to cherish.

terms and places

Abulapak. Dani compound near Gardner's group's camp

Aikhé. River near the Willihiman-Wallalua settlements

akuni. The local people

Anelerak. Ridge near the Willihiman-Wallalua settlements

ap warek. Dead men

Dokolik. One of the traditional battlefields

ebeai. Family house

Elokhera. Local river

etai. Victory dance

etai-eken. "Seeds of singing," a Dani's essence

hakse. Cooking pit

Hellerabet. Major local watchtower

hiperi. Sweet potato

Homaklep. Weyak's village

Homoak. Gardner's group's camp

honai. Men's house

iki palin. Amputation

innumossi. Men's headdress

kain. Strongman or leader

kaio. Watchtower

Libarek. Dance ground

lisé. Long family house

lokop. Type of grass

Lokopalek. A hill village

mawé. Major ceremony of weddings

mikak. Necklaces

Minimo. A village near Wamena

mokat. Ghost

munika. Araucaria seed

nassa. Type of small snail shell used for ornaments

nyeraken aré. Cowrie shell strings

olea. Shelter at the foot of a watchtower

picon. Mouth harp

Puakoloba. Weyak's watchtower

sien. Araucaria tree

sili. Village unit

Siobara. Hill and traditional batttlefield

sué warek. "Dead birds," or captured enemy arms or decoration

Tulem. Missionary station in Wittaia territory

walimoken. Chest ornaments made of snail shells

wam kanekhé. Ceremony for strengthening the holy stones

Wamena. Dutch outpost in the Dani region

Warabara. Hill and traditional battlefield

weem. Battle

Wubarainma. A Willihiman-Wallalua village

wusa. Affected by black magic

yoroik. Mourning dove

people in the text

Abututi. Dani policeman who became a translator for Gardner's group

Aplegma. Dani boy, Weyak's son, frequently filmed by Gardner

Asch, Timothy. Filmmaker and anthropologist, reviewed film and photographic material sent back to the Peabody while Gardner's group was in New Guinea

Brew, J. O. Archaeologist and director of Harvard's Peabody Museum of Archaeology and Ethnology at the time of the making of *Dead Birds*

Bromley, Myron. Christian missionary and expert on Dani languages, whose work Gardner's group used

Broekhuyse, Jan. Dutch anthropologist and district officer in New Guinea who joined Gardner's group to work among the Dani

Chopra, Joyce. Filmmaker who assisted with post-production of *Dead Birds*

Coolidge, Harold. Head of the Pacific Science Board, National Research Council, at the time of the making of *Dead Birds,* corresponded with Gardner prior to the trip

de Bruyn, Victor. Author, anthropologist, and Dutch official in Hollandia, Netherlands New Guinea, who helped Gardner plan his trip to study the Dani

Elisofon, Eliot. Author and *Life Magazine* photographer, briefly a member of Gardner's group in New Guinea

Gerbrands, Adrian A. Dutch author, anthropologist, and expert on indigenous art of South Asia who corresponded with Gardner prior to his trip, worked in the Asmat region in southern New Guinea, and hosted Michael Rockefeller during the first of his two visits to the Asmat

Heider, Karl. Anthropologist, member of Gardner's group, stayed among the Dani to continue research after the others departed, author of *The Dugum Dani* and co-author with Gardner of *Gardens of War*

Jegé Asuk. Young Dani warrior, frequently filmed by Gardner

King, Louis L. Head of the Christian and Missionary Alliance office in New York City at the time of Gardner's trip

Kosi-Alua. Dani clan allied to the Willihiman-Wallalua, who are the main subject of *Dead Birds*

Kurelu. The principal Dani leader in the region where Gardner's group worked, and the name given to the region

Marshall, John. Filmmaker, principal author of *The Hunters,* worked with Gardner at the Film Study Center in the Peabody Museum in the late 1950s

Matthiessen, Peter. Writer and naturalist, member of Gardner's group in New Guinea, where he wrote *Under the Mountain Wall*

Mead, Margaret. Anthropologist, known for fieldwork in Polynesia and her book *Coming of Age in Samoa,* worked out of New York's American Museum of Natural History, met often with Gardner prior to his trip and wrote the introduction to *Gardens of War*

Pospisil, Leopold. Anthropologist at Yale University who had studied and filmed the Kapauku people in New Guinea in the 1950s

Pua. Dani boy, a principal subject of *Dead Birds*

Putnam, Samuel. Close college friend of Michael Rockefeller and briefly a member of Gardner's group in New Guinea, where he accompanied Rockefeller on his first Asmat trip and did photography in the highlands

Rockefeller, Michael. Son of Governor Nelson Rockefeller of New York, joined Gardner's group in New Guinea as a recent Harvard graduate, recorded sound for *Dead Birds* and did still photography, died in a boating accident off the southern coast of New Guinea

Thompson, Carol. Gardner's assistant at the Film Study Center at the time of the making of *Dead Birds*

Uwar. Dani boy frequently filmed by Gardner

Wali. Dani leader who assisted Gardner's group in many ways

Weaké. Dani child murdered by the Wittaia

Weyak. Dani warrior and a principal subject of *Dead Birds*

Willihiman-Wallalua. The Dani clan among whom Gardner's group lived and worked

Wittaia. Dani clan who were traditional enemies of the Willihiman-Wallalua

relevant reading

Benedict, Ruth. *Patterns of Culture*. New York: Houghton Mifflin, 1934.

Bubriski, Kevin. *Michael Rockefeller: New Guinea Photographs, 1961*. Foreword by Robert Gardner. Cambridge, MA: Peabody Museum Press, 2006.

Cassirer, Ernst. *An Essay on Man: An Introduction to a Philosophy of Human Culture*. New Haven: Yale University Press, 1944.

Cavell, Stanley. *The World Viewed: Reflections on the Ontology of Film*. Cambridge, MA: Harvard University Press, 1971; enlarged edition, 1979.

Gardner, Robert. *The Impulse to Preserve: Reflections of a Filmmaker*. New York: Other Press, 2006.

Gardner, Robert, and Karl G. Heider. *Gardens of War: Life and Death in the New Guinea Stone Age*. New York: Random House, 1969.

Gardner, Robert, and Ákos Östör. *Making* Forest of Bliss: *Intention, Circumstance and Chance in Nonfiction Film: A Conversation between Robert Gardner and Ákos Östör*. Cambridge, MA: Harvard Film Archive/Harvard University Press, 2002.

Geertz, Clifford. *The Interpretation of Cultures*. New York: Basic Books, 2000 (1973).

Heider, Karl G. *Ethnographic Film*. Austin: University of Texas Press, 2006 (1976).

Heider, Karl G. *The Dugum Dani: A Papuan Culture in the Highlands of West New Guinea*. New York: Wenner-Gren Foundation for Anthropological Research, 1970.

Heider, Karl G. *The Dani of West Irian: An Ethnographic Companion to the Film* Dead Birds. Berkeley: Warner Modular Publications, Module 2, 1972.

Kluckhohn, Clyde. *Mirror for Man: The Relation of Anthropology to Modern Life*. New York: McGraw-Hill, 1949.

Langer, Susanne. *Philosophy in a New Key: A Study in the Symbolism of Reason, Rite and Art*. Cambridge, MA: Harvard University Press, 1957 (1942).

Lévi-Strauss, Claude. *Tristes Tropiques*. Trans. John and Doreen Weightman, London: Jonathan Cape, 1973 (1955).

Matthiessen, Peter. *Under the Mountain Wall: A Chronicle of Two Seasons in the Stone Age*. New York: Viking Press, 1962.

Meiselas, Susan. *Encounters with the Dani*. New York and Göttingen: International Center of Photography and Steidl, 2003.

Melville, Herman. *Typee: A Romance of the South Seas*. London: John Murray, 1846.

Rockefeller, Michael Clark, and Adrian A. Gerbrands (ed.), *The Asmat of New Guinea: The Journal of Michael Clark Rockefeller*. New York: Museum of Primitive Art, 1967.

Tarkovsky, Andrei. *Sculpting in Time: Reflections on the Cinema.* Trans. Kitty Hunter-Blair, Austin: University of Texas Press, 1987 (1986).

Warren, Charles, editor. *Beyond Document: Essays on Nonfiction Film.* Hanover, NH: Wesleyan University Press and University Press of New England, 1996.

relevant viewing

My selection of the following titles relates in large measure to an early stage in my acquisition of a film sensibility, but they continue to please and instruct on successive viewings. These are not models, but inspirations for my own work.

Brakhage, Stan. *Window Water Baby Moving* (1959).

Buñuel, Luis. *Land Without Bread* (*Las Hurdes,* 1932).

Cartier-Bresson, Henri. *Le Retour* (1945).

Deren, Maya. *A Study in Choreography for Camera* (*Pas de Deux,* 1945).

De Sica, Vittorio. *Bicycle Thieves (Ladri di Biciclette,* 1948).

Dvortsevoy, Sergei. *Paradise* (1996).

Flaherty, Robert. *Man of Aran* (1934).

Franju, Georges. *Blood of the Beasts* (*Le Sang des Bêtes,* 1949).

Gilic, Vlatko. *In Continuo* (1971).

Harris, Hilary. *9 Variations on a Dance Theme* (1966).

Kanevski, Vitaly. *Freeze Die Come to Life* (1989).

Kubelka, Peter. *Unsere Afrikareise* (1966).

Rossellini, Roberto. *Open City (Roma, Città Aperta,* 1945).

Teshigahara, Hiroshi. *Woman in the Dunes* (1964).

Varlamov, Leonid. *Stalingrad* (1943).

Vigo, Jean. *Zero for Conduct (Zéro de Conduite,* 1933).

Wright, Basil. *Song of Ceylon* (1934).

relevant internet sources

http://www.robertgardner.net
http://www.der.org

credits

All materials credited "PM" are in the archives of the Peabody Museum of Archaeology and Ethnology, Harvard University, and are copyright © the President and Fellows of Harvard College.

v	Epigraph from "Of Flesh and Bone" in Isabella Gardner's *The Collected Poems* (Rochester, NY: BOA Editions Ltd., 1990)
vi	Karl Heider, PM2006.17.1.82.26
viii	Jan Broekhuyse, PM2006.15.1.39.20
xviii	Robert Gardner, PM2006.16.1.9.27
2	Courtesy Robert Gardner
4	Isabella Gardner, courtesy Robert Gardner
6	Dale Fruman, courtesy Robert Gardner
7	Dale Fruman, courtesy Robert Gardner
9	Jan Broekhuyse, PM2006.15.1.39.18
10	Eliot Elisofon, PM2006.36.1.71.20
14	Robert Gardner, PM2001.29.343
16	Barbara Roll, courtesy Wilton Dillon
17	Robert Gardner, PM2006.16.1.6.24
20	Samuel Putnam, PM2006.18.1.80.11
24	Courtesy Robert Gardner, gift of Victor de Bruyn
27	Courtesy Robert Gardner
33	Courtesy Robert Gardner
38	Jan Broekhuyse, PM2006.15.1.14.27
41	Karl Heider, PM2006.17.1.79.70
42	Karl Heider, PM2006.17.1.24.12
44	Robert Gardner, PM2006.16.1.21.23
45	Robert Gardner, PM2006.16.1.27.21
47 top left	Karl Heider, PM2006.17.1.79.48
47 top right	Karl Heider, PM2006.17.1.79.62
47 bottom	Courtesy Robert Gardner
49	Michael Rockefeller, PM2006.12.1.140.16
50, 51	Courtesy Robert Gardner
52	Michael Rockefeller, PM accession file 2005.15
53	Michael Rockefeller, PM2006.12.1.4.17
54	Karl Heider, PM2006.17.1.205.25

56	Jan Broekhuyse, PM2006.15.1.46.12
57	Michael Rockefeller, PM2006.12.1.75.25
58	Eliot Elisofon, PM2006.37.1.22.14
59	Robert Gardner, PM2006.16.1.19.1
60	Michael Rockefeller, PM2006.12.1.152.3
62	Karl Heider, PM2006.17.1.81.25
64	Robert Gardner, PM2006.16.1.34.8
67	Robert Gardner, PM2006.16.1.9.27
68	Karl Heider, PM2006.17.1.206.23
70	Eliot Elisofon, PM2006.37.1.14.21
72	Michael Rockefeller, PM2006.12.1.170.27
74	Samuel Putnam, PM2006.18.1.63.3
77	Jan Broekhuyse, PM2006.15.1.58.15
78	Peter Matthiessen, PM2006.14.1.49.5
80 top	Jan Broekhuyse, PM2006.15.1.54.27
80 bottom	Jan Broekhuyse, PM 2006.12.1.157.20
82	Robert Gardner, PM2006.12.1. 48.19
85	Michael Rockefeller , PM2006.12.1.124.25
86	Jan Broekhuyse, PM2006.15.1.64.6
89	Jan Broekhuyse, PM2006.15.1.69.14
91	Courtesy Robert Gardner
93	Courtesy Robert Gardner
94	Eliot Elisofon, PM2006.37.1.59.9
97	Samuel Putnam, PM2006.18.1.64.3
99	Karl Heider, PM2006.17.1.212.32
101	Karl Heider, PM2006.17.1.25.7
102	Robert Gardner, courtesy Robert Gardner
106	Samuel Putnam, PM2006.18.1.55.12
108	Courtesy Robert Gardner
112	Courtesy Robert Gardner
114	Michael Rockefeller, PM2006.12.1.124.14
115	Karl Heider, PM TempID 314.2.14.18
116	Courtesy Robert Gardner
126 top	Courtesy Robert Gardner
126 bottom	Courtesy Robert Gardner
128	Susan Meiselas/Magnum SME3/17(1989)

Acknowledgments

Before any acknowledgments are made, a book like this needs a little explanation. It is unlikely that one nonfiction film, made almost fifty years ago, would be considered at such length and in such conscientious detail in the absence of convincing purpose. Here I will borrow Samuel Johnson's comforting words to help me explain it all. Johnson wrote in his 1765 *Preface to Shakespeare,* "Nothing can please many, and please long, but just representations of general nature." He also said, for the benefit of those still yearning for the world of fancy, "The irregular combinations of fanciful invention may delight a while, by that novelty of which the common satiety of life sends us all in quest; but the pleasures of sudden wonder are soon exhausted, and the mind can only repose on the stability of truth."

I have always taken this assertion to mean that there is virtue not only in writing about actuality, but also in making films about it. So my first acknowledgment is to Dr. Johnson and to these words of his that have sustained me in my search for the repose of which he speaks.

Many others have supported me in a variety of ways, especially my talented friend Charles Warren, who undertook the difficult task of sorting through an immense accumulation of documents covering a major span of time and provenance. He not only sorted, he also found what was required to fashion this filmic chronicle. Giving essential assistance in these matters was Joan K. O'Donnell of the Peabody Museum Press, who never stinted in diligence, encouragement, and intelligence as the book's general editor. I also have enjoyed the wondrous benefits of my designer, Jeannet Leendertse, who makes pages beautiful not just to read but to merely regard.

There are several friends for whom I feel I have undertaken to write this book. Some, like Robert Fulton, Richard Rogers, Robert Lowell, and Jan Lenica, are no longer here to scold or, possibly, give praise, but Ákos Östör, Lina Fruzzetti, and Terry Maltsberger are here, and it is they to whom I look as wardens of my sometimes precarious soul.

Finally, it is, of course, impossible to manage all the handiwork of book writing without associates who care enough to do the many things required. Here I am indebted to three who work at my side at studio7arts: Eric Masunaga, Brian Schwartz, and Lauren DeSantis. I thank also my studio7arts colleagues and close allies in the practice of art: Kevin Bubriski, Robert Fenz, Sharon Lockhart, Samina Quraeshi, Susan Meiselas, and Alex Webb. They set a high standard.